دَفْعُ الْوَيْلِ عَمَّنْ حَطَبَ بِاللَّيْلِ

a bundle of twigs is not a tree

contextualising soundbites from mediaeval scholars used in propaganda to justify indiscriminate killing

compiled by RV, former curator of Islamic mss & prison chaplain

1447/2026

Grosvenor House
Publishing Limited

This book is published by
Grosvenor House Publishing Ltd
Link House
140 The Broadway, Tolworth, Surrey, KT6 7HT.
www.grosvenorhousepublishing.co.uk

A CIP record for this book
is available from the British Library

Paperback ISBN 978-1-83615-410-5
eBook ISBN 978-1-83615-411-2

Bism Allah al-Rahman al-Rahim

In the name of God, the Kind, the Merciful

Contents

About the author

While completing a PhD in Indo-Persian Sufi literature, RV began working at the British Library as a curator of Arabic, editing two volumes of a handlist of manuscripts on Qur'an and Hadith sciences and on Islamic law. There followed a couple of stints living in the Middle East, during which he trained fellow academic and national librarians. Then came a period when he volunteered as an official prison visitor, whilst heading a project taking an archival imaging business from microfilm to online publishing. It was then that he got a "tap on the shoulder" from a mufti who encouraged him to apply to become a Muslim chaplain. An initial seven years with young offenders, including membership of the 'Ibaana' programme that grew out of the Prime Minister's Task Force on Tackling Radicalisation and Extremism,[1] was followed by a further eight years in the long-term, high-security prison estate.

Weaving together strands from across RV's varied academic, professional and pastoral career, this English-language volume is the first in a series of translations from texts plundered by contemporary extremists to radicalise vulnerable fellow Muslims. The intention is eventually, God willing, to publish all of this material in a single Arabic/English bilingual version under the title: *Daf' al-wayl 'amman hataba bil-layl = Repelling the woes of whoever gathering firewood by night goes*.

1 See *Tackling extremism in the UK*, December 2013 https://www.gov.uk/government/publications/tackling-extremism-in-the-uk-report-by-the-extremism-taskforce (viewed 27/05/2025)

Note on the translation & transliteration

Occasionally, it has been necessary in the translation to insert words in order to better convey the meaning of the Arabic text. Instead of using the academic convention of [square brackets], a lighter grey font is used for any inserted words. This is because, after over a decade and a half of working with Muslim and other young offenders and high-security prisoners, I have come to realise that [square brackets] confuse rather than assist lower-ability readers, while those fortunate enough to be of a higher ability have no difficulty whatever convention is used, so long as it is applied consistently.

Regarding the transliteration, I have made use of the Library of Congress romanisation scheme with which I became familiar in previous jobs as a curator of Arabic manuscripts and printed materials. However, I have avoided diacritics for the same reason as I have avoided the use of square brackets.

If you are able to compare the translation with the Arabic text, you will find that, for variety, the Arabic verb *qala*, which literally means 'said', is also rendered 'asked', 'answered', 'replied', 'explained', 'exclaimed', etc., in English.

Note on the content

Finally, in what has become a commonplace practice today, it seems not inappropriate to remind readers that the content of this book is drawn chiefly from mediaeval legal texts. As such, they will find that some of the views and opinions expressed in the translations are not in accord with 21st-century British values.

Introduction

This short work's title, *A bundle of dry twigs is not a living tree*, was inspired by combining a simile in the Qur'an that describes a good word as a healthy, fruit-bearing tree (Q.14:24-25) with a metaphor in a sentence that an Andalusian scholar, Ibn al-'Arabi (d.543/1148), wrote in his treatise on abrogating and abrogated verses, *al-Nasikh wa-al-mansukh fi al-Qur'an*:

> "Of the masters of authorship who have collated data on this topic, not one remains who has not gathered firewood by night, dragging this field of knowledge by the tail till it is worthy of lament or, say, 'woe'."

The idiomatic phrase "gathering firewood by night" refers to the actions of those who, because they are enveloped in darkness, cannot tell what exactly they're picking up from the ground beneath them. This is what happens when unscholarly Muslims pick pithy phrases from a database of mediaeval Arabic-Islamic texts. Some such Muslims, no doubt, are sincere, imagining out of ignorance that each phrase encapsulates a general Islamic legal principle on jihad and on the lawfulness of the killing of disbelievers. Others are cynical extremist firebrands, deliberately intending to dupe the vulnerable into becoming the unwitting tools of their violent ideological bigotry.

This book takes a bundle of firewood gathered nocturnally by Daesh propagandists, who passed it by social media to the gullible victims of their radicalisation; and it painstakingly matches each dry twig with the centuries-old tree from which it came.

The decontextualised 'soundbites' from mediaeval Islamic texts that comprise this "bundle of dry twigs" was, I learned, first published at a list in the Daesh online magazine *Dabiq*. They were copied out for me by a young brother who said that he wanted to understand what rebuttal, if any, a 'government imam' (i.e. a Muslim prison chaplain) could provide to their combined thrust, which ostensibly justifies the plotting and perpetrating of indiscriminate killing of non-Muslims in our country. However, obtaining these soundbites wasn't quite that straightforward.

What actually happened was this. First, the young man spoke to a colleague of mine, telling him that he'd read that, in his commentary on the Qur'an, a respected mediaeval Muslim scholar, al-Qurtubi (d.671/1273), had written that the ruling in the Sword Verse (Q.9:5) to fight, besiege, ambush and kill pagan Arab associators[2] abrogated all earlier divine commands to show clemency and generosity towards non-Muslims. My colleague mentioned this to me. Having previously read and translated the relevant section of the commentary in question, I saw an opportunity to rework it in a way that might benefit not only that individual, but also other Muslims who might have already been – or in future be – exposed to that incorrect opinion and led astray. Included in this introduction is the text of my reflection. It was only after reading that and discovering that it was I who had written it, that the young man approached me with his list of twenty-one soundbites in English, which he asked me to rebut.

Armed with the names of the scholars and the titles of their works, I set about finding the sources of each of the soundbites in the *Maktaba Shamela* database (https://shamela.ws) by searching for the Arabic equivalents of selected English keywords. After that, he and I sat together in one-to-one sessions, during which I would translate orally the context of the soundbites. That continued for a few weeks until circumstances meant that he moved elsewhere, and so our sessions had to stop. However, by then I had realised the potential of this material to assist if not in deradicalising fellow Muslims who had become committed extremists, then at least to intellectually 'vaccinate' those vulnerable to their wiles. So, I began to translate the whole of each fatwa or chapter from which the soundbites had been taken.

What will soon become clear is that, even in English, the mostly legal texts from which the soundbites were taken are too complicated for most readers to understand, especially those with limited literacy or concentration. With the longer fatwas, as you will discover, one often has to trudge through many pages to find the sentence chosen by the propagandists. On top of that, it turns out that many of the sections, fatwas or chapters have no direct

2 i.e. idolaters. I have chosen to use the word 'associator' in this book as it best matches the Arabic term *mushrik*, which means someone who engages in *shirk*, the practice of associating anything with God in divinity.

relevance to war and fighting. Insofar as they do relate to war, they refer to hostile enemy combatants in battle, not to civilians peacefully going about their day-to-day business in the street, on public transport, in office blocks, concert halls or shopping malls in a multicultural and multifaith society like Great Britain. And the fact that most of the soundbites aren't drawn specifically from those sections entitled *Kitab al-Jihad* in legal manuals suggests that the Daesh propagandists who compiled the list most probably found them by searching for keyword in the same Arabic database as I did, rather than by a detailed academic study of the laws of war.

In this collection of translated soundbites selected by Daesh propagandists, each of their soundbites appears in capital letters[3] at the top in a HANDWRITING-STYLE FONT and again – but in lower case – in the context from which it was taken. Where it is not absolutely obvious that the selected soundbite is drawn from the longer Arabic text, it will instead appear in a footnote. Likewise, if the soundbite clearly fits the context, but the translation either appears too literal or adds words that are not in the original text, then a more accurate sense-for-sense translation is given in the footnotes. Finally, as in the eleventh soundbite from al-Shawkani's *al-Sayl al-jarrar*, a footnote explains how it may be that the Daesh propagandist's mistranslation of the Arabic *lam yu'man* ("he has no guarantee of safe passage") as *lam yu'min* ("he has not believed") is an unintentional grammatical mistake due to a prejudiced misreading of the text rather than deliberate misrepresentation of it.

3 The use of capitals is to replicate the handwritten format in which I was given them.

What prompted the soundbites to be transcribed

TALKING ABOUT JIHAD FOR A CHANGE

to stop it being misunderstood and misrepresented

"Hajj and jihad go on until the Last Hour under those Muslims, righteous or shameless, who are in positions of authority. Nothing can nullify or abolish either of them."

> In an authentic hadith, Ibn 'Abbas reported that the Prophet PBUH said, "Isn't the cure for ignorance to ask?"
>
> (*Sunan Ibn Majah*)

This is standard Sunni doctrine, taken from *al-'Aqidah al-Tahawiyah*. Since jihad is a core part of our faith, it's essential we understand it well enough so that we don't wrong ourselves and others either by acting as if jihad didn't exist, or by claiming it is whatever we want it to be. If you don't know, ask.

Recently, I was shown some handwritten "Questions for the imam" to explain words based on the Qur'an & Sunnah, and also from scholars. First was the claim that, in the Sword Verse (Q.9:5), Allah ordered Muslims to kill all 'kuffar' wherever they find them, and next that al-Qurtubi wrote in his commentary *al Jami' li-ahkam al-Qur'an* that this verse abrogated all other verses in the Qur'an that refer to having peaceful relations with non-Muslims. Yes, al-Qurtubi did write this in his commentary. But is it his opinion? And, if not, did he agree with it?

In the column on the right is a translation of what al Qurtubi actually wrote. So, judge for yourself. RV

WHAT AL-QURTUBI WROTE IN CONTEXT:

"Thereafter [scholars] have differed. al-Husayn ibn al-Fadl said, 'This abrogates every verse in the Qur'an that mentions turning away from, or being patient in the face of, harm from enemies.' However, al-Dahhak, al Suddi and 'Ata' said, 'It is abrogated by His saying (Q.47:4) *{thereafter either be magnanimous* or ransom}*; and since captives are not to be killed in cold blood, they may either be shown magnanimity or may be ransomed.' Mujahid and Qatadah said, 'Rather it abrogates His saying *{thereafter either be magnanimous or ransom}*; and concerning captives from the associators, only slaying is permitted.' However, Ibn Zayd said, 'Both verses remain binding'; and this is the correct [opinion], as magnanimity, execution and ransom appeared in Allah's Messenger's PBUH rulings on them from the very first war against them, namely the Battle of Badr, as stated above."

WHOEVER CANNOT FIND A GOOD QUR'AN COMMENTARY TO READ should read the life of the Prophet PBUH, because "His nature was the Qur'an."

The fact that al-Qurtubi & others quoted the words of al-Husayn ibn al-Fadl isn't proof that he was right, only that he said it. It's an opinion al-Qurtubi used to introduce the correct view that the lawful Muslim ruler may order whichever option best fits the circumstances, based on intelligence.

It's misleading to say without any explanation that al-Qurtubi, one of Islam's best-known scholars, wrote it in his commentary. If we read what he wrote in context, it soon becomes obvious that he disagreed with al-Husayn ibn al-Fadl's opinion. Part of al-Qurtubi's evidence is these words (Q.47:4) *{thereafter either be magnanimous or ransom}*, which came down before the command to *{kill all associators wherever you find them...}* in *Surat al-Tawbah* (Q.9). Had the command to kill abrogated every verse relating to patience & mercy, we'd have expected the Prophet PBUH to have become totally ruthless after it was revealed. But he PBUH didn't.

As al-Qurtubi wrote about Allah's command in Q.9:5, "[linguistically] *{then slay the associators}* is general on every associator. However, as explained earlier in *Surat al-Baqarah*, the Sunnah made exceptions of women, monks, children and others..."

After the command to kill associators *{wherever you find them}*, in the very next verse (Q.9:6) Allah revealed *{& if an associator asks your protection, grant him protection so that he may hear Allah's Word, then take him to his place of safety; this is because they are people who do not know.}* On this, al-Qurtubi quotes Imam Malik, who said, "If an enemy fighter is found roaming in Muslim lands, and he says, 'I've come to seek safety,' cases like this are suspect, but my view is that he should be taken to his place of safety," which is defined in al-Baghawi's *tafsir* as "that place where he feels secure, which is his people's home country."

A few years ago, a young brother worked all this out for himself after I'd lent him Adil Salahi's 854-page biography of the Prophet PBUH to read. In his second week on basic IEP for fighting another brother, he'd already read half the book when he arrived at my Islamic class, excited to pass on his new insight. "Brothers, brothers, brothers," he said, "there's something I have to tell you. You can't understand the Qur'an unless you know about the life of the Prophet PBUH." When he'd finished the book, I reminded him of what he'd said in class, and then I asked him what he thought, now he'd got his TV back, seeing on the news atrocities done in the name of our Islamic faith. "It's a joke, isn't it?" he told me, "If Islam was like that, nobody would believe it."

Do you really want to understand the Qur'an? If so, don't just repeat bits of verses or single sentences taken out of context from a translation or a commentary because they fit your purpose. Read the whole of the Qur'an, then read it again and again. And if you can't find a commentary, then reading the life of the Prophet PBUH will help you to understand God's revelation because, as 'A'ishah said, "His nature was the Qur'an." RV

How the soundbites were transcribed

Impressed by the reflection above, a radicalised Muslim brother transcribed for me by hand in capital letters, with the blank lines at the top and bottom and a gap in the middle, the soundbites that he said had convinced him to conspire and act.

> PROPHET MUHAMMED (SAW) SAID, "THE KAFIR & HIS KILLER WILL NEVER MEET IN HELLFIRE."-SAHIH MUSLIM/ABU DAWUD
>
> IMAM SHAFI (R) SAID, "THE LAND OF DARUL HARB IS PERMISSIBLE FOR A MUSLIM TO VIOLATE THE BLOOD & WEALTH THEREIN BECAUSE IT IS A LAND OF SHIRK."-AL UMM / AT TABARI (R) SAID, "THE IJMA IS THAT THE RULING OF ALLAH ON THE HARBI MUSHRIKEEN IS THAT THEY ARE TO BE KILLED."-TAFSIR TABARI / IBN TAYMIYAH (R) SAID, "CONCERNING THE MUSLIMS WHO ENTER DARUL HARB, LIKEWISE IF HE KIDNAPS THEM OR THEIR CHILDREN, OR SUBDUES THEM IN ANY WAY, THEN THE LIFE & WEALTH OF THE HARBI KUFFAR ARE PERMISSIBLE FOR THE MUSLIM, SO IF THEY SEIZE THEM IN A SHARI MANNER, THEY OWN THEM."-MAJMU ALFATAWA / IBN TAYMIYAH (R) SAID, "KUFR ALONGSIDE MUHARABAH IS PRESENT IN EVERY KAFIR, SO IT IS PERMITTED TO ENSLAVE HIM, AS IT IS PERMITTED TO KILL HIM."-MAJMU ALFATAWA / SHAWKANI (R) SAID, "IT IS ALLOWED FOR THE MUSLIM WHO ENTERS DARUL HARB (WITH AN AMAN FROM ITS PEOPLE) TO TAKE WHATEVER HE IS ABLE OF THEIR WEALTH & TO SHED WHATEVER HE IS ABLE TO OF THEIR BLOOD."-ASSAYLALJARRAR / SAHNUN (R) SAID, "& IF A PEOPLE IN DARUL HARB EMBRACE ISLAM, IT IS PERMISSIBLE FOR THEM TO KILL WHOEVER THEY CAN & TAKE THEIR WEALTH."-AN NAWADIR WA-ZIYADAT / IBN QUDAMAH (R) SAID, "THERE IS NO QISAS FOR THE ONE WHO KILLS A HARBI KAFIR, DUE TO THE STATEMENT OF ALLAH, {THEN KILL THE POLYTHEISTS WHEREVER YOU FIND THEM}, NOR FOR THE ONE WHO KILLS A MURTAD & BECAUSE HE IS ONE WHOSE BLOOD IS PERMISSIBLE TO BE SHED, HE IS MORE RESEMBLING OF THE HARBI KAFIR."-AL KAFI FI FIQH AL-IMAM AHMED / IMAM SHAAFI (R) SAID, "ALLAH MADE THE BLOOD & WEALTH OF THE KAFIR LAWFUL UNLESS HE PAYS THE JIZYA OR IS GIVEN A COVENANT OF SECURITY FOR A PERIOD OF TIME."-AL UMM / IMAM SHAAFI (R) SAID, "& THE KAFIR'S BLOOD IS NOT SPARED UNTIL HE BECOMES A MUSLIM."-AL UMM/ SHAWKANI (R) SAID, "THE KAFIR, WHETHER HE FIGHTS THE MUSLIM OR NOT, HIS BLOOD IS HALAL TO SPILL AS LONG AS HE IS A KAFIR."-ASSAYLALJARRAR / IBN HAJAR (R) SAID, "IT IS THE EXISTENCE OF KUFR THAT PERMITS THE BLOOD."-FATHULBAARI / IMAM QURTUBI (R) SAID, IF A MUSLIM MEETS A KAFIR WHO HAS NO COVENANT, IT IS PERMISSIBLE FOR HIM TO KILL HIM."-TAFSIR QURTUBI IMAM ABU HANIFA (R) SAID, "REGARDING A HARBI KAFIR WHO IS KILLED BY A MUSLIM, THERE IS NO RETALIATION (AGAINST THE KILLER) & THE DIYAH IS NOT TO BE PAID, BECAUSE THE BLOOD OF THE KAFIR IS HALAL (TO SHED) UNLESS IT IS ESTABLISHED THAT HE HAS A COVENANT OR IS UNDER DHIMMAH."-AL HAWI AL KABIR / IBN MUFLIH (R) SAID, "THERE IS NO EXPIATION, NO BLOOD MONEY PAID FOR KILLING A KAFIR THAT HAS NO PEACE TREATY, BECAUSE HIS BLOOD IS GENERALLY HALAL (TO SPILL) LIKE THE PIG."-AL MUBDI/ IBN QUDAMAH (R) SAID ABOUT THE HARBI KAFIR, "SHEDDING HIS BLOOD IS HALAL WITHOUT EXCEPTION, JUST LIKE SWINE."-AL MUGHNI / IBN HAZM (R) SAID, "& IT IS HALAL TO KILL ANYONE OTHER THAN THOSE MENTIONED (WOMEN & KIDS) OF THE MUSHRIKEEN, BOTH THE COMBATANT & NON-COMBATANT, THE BUSINESSMAN & THE EMPLOYED, THE ELDERLY MAN WHETHER OR NOT HE IS A PERSON OF INFLUENCE, THE FARMER, THE BISHOP OR PRIEST OR MONK, THE BLIND OF CRIPPLE, NO ONE IS GIVEN EXCEPTION."-AL MUHALLA / UMAR BIN KHATTAB (R) SAID, ENCOURAGING ABU JANDAL TO KILL HIS OWN FATHER, SUHAYL IBN AMR, "BE PATIENT, ABU JANDAL, FOR THEY ARE MERELY MUSHRIKEEN & THEIR BLOOD IS NOTHING BUT LIKE THE BLOOD OF A DOG."-AHMED /
>
> IMAM SHAYBANI (R) SAID, "& TO ATTACK THEM WITH FIRE & CATAPULTS & THIS INCLUDES DEMOLISHING THEIR HOMES & THROWING SNAKES & SCORPIONS UPON THEM EVEN IF WOMEN & CHILDREN ARE AMONGST THEM. "-SHARH MIHNAJ / IBN QASIM (R) SAID, "& IT IS PERMITTED TO FIRE UPON THE KUFFAR WITH CATAPULTS, EVEN IF WOMEN, CHILDREN, OLD MEN & MONKS ARE KILLED UNINTENTIONALLY, BECAUSE OF THE IJMA CONCERNING THE PERMISSIBILITY OF TERRORISING THEM." / IBN RUSHD (R) SAID, "TERRORISING IS PERMITTED BY IJMA AGAINST ALL TYPES OF KUFFAR. "-AL HASHIYA ALA RAWDH

If this is the only page that you read in this book, without any of the context, you will most likely to end up misguided.

Soundbite 1: "The kafir and his killer will never meet in hellfire."

PROPHET MUHAMMED (SAW) SAID, "THE KAFIR & HIS KILLER WILL NEVER MEET IN HELLFIRE."-SAHIH MUSLIM/ABU DAWUD[4]

C1/1 Chapter on whoever kills a disbeliever then strives to do what is right[5]

C1/2 His PBUH saying, *"The kafir and his killer will never meet in hellfire,"* or, in another narration, "will not both be brought together in a way where one may harm the other." Someone said, "Who are they, O Messenger of Allah?" He PBUH replied, "A believer who kills a disbeliever then strives to do what is right."[6]

C1/3 Regarding the first narration, al-Qadi[7] said, "It may be that this is specific to whoever kills a disbeliever in jihad, and that act becomes an atonement for his sins, so that he is not punished for them; alternatively, it may be due to a particular intention or situation. It may also be that his punishment, if the believer is punished, is by means other than the Fire, such as: [1] being held back at first in the area of the ramparts between Paradise and Hell from entering Paradise,[8] and so not enter the Fire; or [2]

4 See https://shamela.ws/book/1711/2847 (viewed 29/04/2025) for the Arabic text of *Bab man qatala kafiran thumma saddada*.

5 For those unfamiliar with Islamic jurisprudence, legal arguments are normally based on quotations from the principal sources of the Sharia, namely the Qur'an and the Sunnah of the Prophet PBUH, before progressing to any scholarly consensus and reasoned analogy. The list, as it was given to me, begins with an authentic hadith, perhaps for this very reason, before proceeding to quote from mediaeval scholars' works. This excerpt is from al-Nawawi's commentary on *al-Minhaj sharh Sahih Muslim ibn al-Hajjaj*.

6 There is a hadith (no. 3007), classed as authentic by Muhammad Nasir al-Din al-Albani in his *Sahih al-targhib wa-al-tarhib*, which narrated by the companion 'Amr ibn al-Hamiq from the Prophet PBUH, who said: "Any man who guarantees the safety of another man over his lifeblood then kills him, I am innocent of the killer, even if the victim is a disbeliever." The issue of guarantees of safety, how the safety guaranteed by one Muslim is binding on all others, and safety does not need to be explicitly stated but can be implied and still binding.

7 Imam al-Nawawi here is paraphrasing the relevant section from al-Qadi 'Iyad ibn Musa al-Yahsubi's (d.544/1149) commentary, *Ikmal al-mu'lim bi-fawa'id Muslim*; and later scholars have tended to quote al-Nawawi's paraphrase rather than referring back to al-Qadi's original text. (See https://shamela.ws/book/122406/3498 - viewed 29/04/2025)

8 Mention of "the ramparts between Paradise and Hell" appears in the sura of that name, *Surat al-A'raf* (Q. 7:46-48) {*& between them both, the people of Paradise and of Hell, is a veil; and, on the ramparts between the two, there are men who recognise each of the people Paradise and of Hell by*

if he is punished by means of the Fire, it will be in a place other than where the disbelievers are punished, and so they are not both brought together in any of its levels." He went on to say, "As for his PBUH saying in the second narration, '... brought together in a way where one harms the other,' it points to its being a particular type of bringing together." He then said, "It is a problem of semantics; and the soundest position is that its meaning is as we indicated, namely that they are not brought together at one time, if the believer deserves to be punished, so that the disbeliever may taunt him for entering the Fire with him, and that his faith did not benefit him, nor did his killing him; and words like this appear in some hadiths." However, his PBUH saying in this hadith "A believer who kills a disbeliever then strives to do what is right"[9] is problematic because a believer, when he strives to do what is right, meaning is steadfast on the ideal path, and does not mix evil deeds in with his good deeds, he ought not to enter the Fire at all, regardless of whether he killed a disbeliever or not. On this, al-Qadi said, "For me, his PBUH purpose in saying 'then strives to do what is right' refers back to the disbelieving killer and is in line with the meaning of the previous hadith, 'Allah laughs over two men, one of whom kills the other, who both enter Paradise.' Some scholars have considered the fact that, according to some narrators, this expression changes, and that its correct version relates to a believer whom a disbeliever kills,[10] and 'then that disbeliever strives to do what is right.' As for the meaning of his PBUH saying 'they will not both be brought together

---

their mark, and they call out to the people of Paradise 'Peace be upon you'; they do not enter Paradise despite longing to do so...}.

9 This calls to mind the hadith (no. 6914) in *Sahih al-Bukhari*, narrated by 'Abd Allah ibn 'Amr, in which the Prophet PBUH said, "Whoever kills a non-Muslim protected by covenant shall not smell the scent of Paradise, even though its scent wafts out for a travelling distance of forty years." Of course, the Qur'an and Sunnah teach us that sincere repentance can change this outcome. However, a prerequisite of one's repentance being accepted is to acknowledge that one has sinned, and there is little, if any, evidence that those who selected these twenty-one decontextualised soundbites were concerned to warn their intended readers of the possibility, let alone the perils, of unlawfully killing non-Muslims.

10 The translator understands that, due to Arabic grammar, it is possible to interpret the phrase *mu'min qatala kafiran* in the hadith in two ways: 1. a believer who kills a disbeliever; and 2. a believer who kills whilst he is still a disbeliever, before later becoming a believer. It is to this second, less obvious interpretation that al-Nawawi's quotation from al-Qadi 'Iyad refers.

in a way where one harms the other,' it is that they will not enter it for the purpose of punishment; and this would be an exception in terms of coming together on arrival and their arguing on the bridge to Hell." This is the last of al-Qadi's words on this issue.

Soundbite 2: "The land of Darul Harb is permissible..."

IMAM SHAFI (R) SAID, "THE LAND OF DARUL HARB IS PERMISSIBLE FOR A MUSLIM TO VIOLATE THE BLOOD & WEALTH THEREIN BECAUSE IT IS A LAND OF SHIRK." -AL UMM[11]

C2/1 The situation of Muslims fighting an enemy among whom there are their Muslim children

C2/2 Abu Hanifah – Allah have mercy on him – said, "If the Muslims besiege their enemy, and the enemy take to their ramparts with Muslim children as human shields," he said, "the Muslims should shoot arrows and catapults at them, intent thereby on killing the people of war, and not intending thereby the Muslim children."[12] Al-Awza'i said, "The Muslims should hold back from shooting at them, but if any of the enemy stands out, they should shoot at him, for Allah – exalted and glorified – says (Q.48:25) *{If it had not been for believing men and believing women}* till the verse ends.[13] So, how can Muslims shoot at associators whom they cannot see?" Abu Yusuf – Allah have mercy on him – said on this, "al-Awza'i interpreted this verse in a contrary way. If it had been forbidden to shoot at associators and fight them whenever they had Muslim children with them, that would also have been forbidden if they had had their own women and children with them, because Allah's Messenger PBUH forbade the killing of women, children, and adolescents, and yet

11 See https://shamela.ws/book/1655/2122 (viewed 29/04/2025) for the Arabic text of *Hal al-Muslimin yuqatiluna al-'aduw wa-fihim atfaluhum* in Imam al-Shafi'i in *Kitab al-Umm*.

12 For comparison, according to Chapter 4, para. 6 of *A soldier's guide to the law of armed conflict* (Army Code 71130, issue 5.0: February 2005) on the rules of combat for British armed forces, "Civilians should be removed from the vicinity of military objectives so far as possible, and the belligerents should endeavour to avoid siting their military installations near the civilian population. Failures by the defenders in this regard should not inhibit attacking commanders from attacking military objectives though they must, as always, take feasible precautions to minimize civilian casualties and damage."

13 The whole of Q.48:25, which relates to the events round the signing of the treaty of al-Hudaybiyah, reads *{It is they who disbelieved and barred you from the Sacred Mosque, with the offering kept from reaching its place of sacrifice. If it had not been for believing men and believing women whom you do not know, whom you might have crushed, and so have unwittingly been afflicted by great shame because of them, but you held back so that Allah might cause whomever He willed to enter into His mercy. If the believers and disbelievers had been separated from each other, We would have inflicted a painful punishment on those of them who had disbelieved.}*

Allah's Messenger PBUH besieged the people of Taif, the people of Khaybar, and the tribes of Quraydah and al-Nadir. According to the reports that have reached us, the Muslims acquired the most powerful weapons that they could against them; and it has reached us that the Prophet PBUH aimed catapults at the people of Taif. If it had been necessary for Muslims to hold back from attacking the associators if there were children in their midst, then Allah's Messenger PBUH would have prohibited killing them. They would not have fought because their squares and fortresses are never devoid of children, women, feeble old men, the young, prisoners, merchants, as was the case in Taif and elsewhere, famously preserved in the Sunnah and biography of Allah's Messenger PBUH; and thereafter the Muslims and the pious predecessors of Muhammad's PBUH companions continued acting likewise against the fortresses of non-Arabs before us. And on that basis, it has not reached us that any of them held back from shooting or using any other force at a fortress due to the presence of women and children, and the presence of whomsoever it is not lawful to kill amongst those who were apparent amongst them.

C2/3 Al-Shafi'i – Allah have mercy on him – said, "As for the basis of the argument in relation to the killing associators when there are children, women and monks among them, and whoever else he PBUH forbade the killing of, Allah's Messenger PBUH launched a raid on Banu al-Mustaliq when they were with their livestock in pasture; and he was asked about the people of a settlement who are attacked at night, and some of their women and children are among those wounded or killed. He replied, 'They are of them,' by which he PBUH meant that the land of Darul Harb is permissible for a Muslim to violate the blood and wealth therein because it is a land of Shirk.[14] Shedding blood is prohibited on the basis of faith,

14 Or, "... shedding blood in that land is permitted, because it is part of the land of idolatry, and fighting associators is permitted." See https://shamela.ws/book/1655/2128 (viewed 29/04/2025) for the Arabic text of *al-Dar mubahah li-annaha dar shirk wa-qital al-mushrikin mubah*. As what follows on immediately make clear, this sentence must not be taken as a licence from the Prophet PBUH to kill indiscriminately in non-Muslim countries but rather, in a formally declared war, as a legal and moral defence where noncombatants are killed unintentionally, analogous to what was quoted in the footnote above from *A soldier's guide to the law of armed conflict* on the rules of combat for British armed forces.

whether the believer was in the land of war or the land of faith.[15] Allah the Exalted has imposed reparations regarding a believer, if he is killed.[16] Attacks should not be launched against a settlement, if it is a land of Islam or a land of safety with a treaty that the Muslims have entered into.[17] No one has the right to attack it, rather he has the right to go after whoever's blood it is lawful to shed without attacking that land. As regards women and children, although he PBUH forbade killing them, shedding their blood is not prohibited due to the acceptance of Islam or their parents' acceptance of Islam; nor, indeed, is shedding their blood prohibited due to the land itself being prohibited. We have sought to show that the Prophet PBUH only forbade killing them by targeting them in particular, if their location is known. And if anyone asks, "What proof is there of that?" the response is that, in his PBUH own leading of attacks or ordering of attacks and of those leading attacks, he PBUH did not abstain absolutely from causing such losses. Likewise, his PBUH saying "They are of them," means that no reparations are due in relation to them, in other words that they are not protected due to acceptance of Islam or due to the land they live in. and Muslims do not differ, as far as I know, that no reparations are due from whoever harms them in an attack. As for a Muslim, shedding his blood is forbidden wherever he may be. Whoever harms another Muslim has sinned by so doing, if he did so deliberately; and retribution is due from him, if he knew him to be a Muslim and harmed him deliberately. Reparations are due, if he did not know him to be a Muslim, the reason being that the prohibition of the blood of a

---

15 Note also Imam al-Shafi'i's well-known maxim in *Kitab al-Umm*, that he describes as "consistent with revelation, the Sunnah, and what Muslims comprehend and are in consensus over: Whatever is lawful in the abode of Islam is lawful in the land of disbelief. Whatever is forbidden in the land of Islam is forbidden in the land of disbelief."

16 See Q.4:92 *{It is not right for a believer to kill a believer except by mistake. Whoever kills a believer by mistake, then freeing a believing slave is required and paying compensation to his next of kin, unless they waive that right out of charity. If the victim is from a people who are hostile to you, and he is a believer, then freeing a believing slave. If the victim is from a people between you and whom there is a covenant, then a compensation paid to his next of kin and the freeing of a believing slave. Whoever cannot find the means to pay, fasting two consecutive months is required from Allah by way of repentance. Allah has always been Omniscient, Wise.}*

17 To abide by Imam al-Shafi'i's logic, Muslims today must either treat almost the entire world as falling into these two categories, or else deem any treaties invalid because one believes that every Muslim who entered into them with non-Muslims is an apostate.

Muslim is different from the prohibition of the blood of a non-Muslim child or woman, because the killing of those two was forbidden due to Allah's will. Our considered opinion – and Allah the Exalted knows best – is that those two categories, women and children, were forbidden him PBUH since their changing and becoming slaves is more beneficial than killing them, as they have no means of causing harm that they should both be killed for it. So, enslaving them is better than killing them.[18]

C2/4 As for al-Awza'i's interpretation, it may be as he interpreted it to be, or it may be that his withholding from attacking them is due to his prior knowledge that a group of them had already willingly accepted Islam. We prefer to act on what al-Awza'i said if there is no dire need for us to fight the inhabitants of a fortress, or if we have the ability not to fight the inhabitants of some other fortress. If there are no Muslims amongst them, they can be left; and if there are Muslims amongst them then it is more magnanimous as well as closest to keeping oneself safe from sinning by harming the Muslims amongst them. However, if we are compelled to because we fear for our own lives by holding back from waging war against them, then we would fight them without deliberately killing any Muslim. If we were to harm a Muslim, then we would atone for it. As long as there is no dire necessity, abandoning fighting them is closest to keeping oneself safe from sin, and hence it is preferable to me.[19]

18 Imam al-Shafi'i makes it clear that this notion that non-believing women and children should be spared because of their value as slaves is not based on any scriptural text, but merely a personal opinion that he has reached. The Qur'an, however, points to the sanctity of human life generally (Q.5:32) *{For this reason, We decreed for the Israelites that whoever takes a life other than in lawful retribution for a life, or to wreak havoc in the land, then it is as though he has slain all humanity; and whoever saves a life, it is as though he has saved all humanity. Our messengers came to them with clear evidence, but since that time many of them have gone to excess in the land.}*

19 As with all the Daesh propagandists' soundbites, one must ponder on whether is accurately reflects the thrust of the context from which it was taken.

Soundbite 3: "The *ijma'* is that ... the *harbi mushrikeen* ... are to be killed."

AT TABARI (R) SAID, "THE IJMA IS THAT THE RULING OF ALLAH ON THE HARBI MUSHRIKEEN IS THAT THEY ARE TO BE KILLED." -TAFSIR TABARI[20]

C3/1 There is, in Allah's saying (Q.5:34) *{except those who repent before you can capture them}*,[21] a clear indication for whoever has understanding that the ruling mentioned by Allah – Glorious and Mighty – in relation to brigands applies to Muslims and those non-Muslims with a covenant as distinct from those associators who have declared war on the Muslims. That is because if the ruling were about those enemies from the associators as opposed to the Muslims and those non-Muslims under their protection, it would have required that their Islam, when they accepted Islam or repented after we had captured them, would not have caused to lapse whatever was their due in terms of killings prior to their accepting Islam and repenting, and whatever the Muslims were due regarding enemies amongst the associators. **According to Muslim consensus, the fact is that the acceptance of Islam by an enemy associator after being captured by Muslims removes any penalty from him just as it would before being captured**;[22] and that is what points to the correctness of the statement of whoever says that Allah meant by the verse on brigands in this context, the brigands of the people of our religion or under our protection, as opposed to anyone other than them from the associators of hostile nations.

---

20 See https://shamela.ws/book/43/5554 - viewed 29/04/2025) for the Arabic text of *wa-fi qawlihi {illa alladhina tabu min qabl an taqdiru 'alayhim} dalil wadih li-man wafaqa li-*.

21 This excerpt is the closest in meaning to the English wording presented by Daesh propagandists. It appears, in fact, to be not a quotation, but a paraphrase of part of al-Tabari's commentary on this verse, the implication of which is that the default position in the Sharia for hostile [able-bodied adult male] people who associate anything with God in divinity is that they be killed. The verse in question, as the commentator clearly felt the need to point out in his day – as, indeed, we do in ours – does not provide a justification for the indiscriminate killing of any non-Muslims in foreign lands.

22 Or, as the Daesh propagandists appear to have paraphrased it, "The *ijma'* is that the ruling of Allah on the *harbi mushrikeen* is that they are to be killed."

Soundbite 4: "Concerning the Muslims who enter Darul Harb..."

IBN TAYMIYAH (R) SAID, "CONCERNING THE MUSLIMS WHO ENTER DARUL HARB, LIKEWISE IF HE KIDNAPS THEM OR THEIR CHILDREN, OR SUBDUES THEM IN ANY WAY, THEN THE LIFE & WEALTH OF THE HARBI KUFFAR ARE PERMISSIBLE FOR THE MUSLIM, SO IF THEY SEIZE THEM IN A SHARI MANNER, THEY OWN THEM."-MAJMU ALFATAWA[23]

C4/1 Ibn Taymiyah was asked about a person from among the disbelievers in the lands of the disbelievers who was in debt and sold himself to a Muslim and took the price, settling his debt with it, and who also sold his daughter; and they accepted enslavement. However, the Muslim merchant incurred a loss over their travel, subsistence, and clothing costs until they arrived in the lands of Islam. Is it permissible to buy or sell them?[24]

C4/2 So, he responded: "If the Muslim entered the land of war without a guarantee of safety, bought their children, and took them with him to the land of Islam, they would be his property, by the agreement of the four imams; and he would have the right to sell them to Muslims, and Muslims would be allowed to buy from him. The seller would have the right to the whole price from the buyer. Likewise, if a resident of the land of war were to sell himself to a Muslim, who took him with him to the land of Islam, then he would be the Muslim's property according to the most appropriate understanding. However, what if they were to give the Muslim their children gratis, and he were to take them with him to the land of Islam, then how about if they were to sell that to him?

23 See https://shamela.ws/book/7289/14478 (viewed 29/04/2025) for Arabic text of Ibn Taymiyah's response to *wa-su'ila 'an shakhs min al-kuffar fi bilad al-kuffar kana 'alayhi dayn*.

24 As with so many of these quotations selected by Daesh propagandists, it is clear from the question that Ibn Taymiyah was not asked for a general ruling on the Sharia-compliance of Muslims living in safety outside Muslim lands killing non-Muslim and/or seizing them, their children and goods; rather, he was asked specifically about the lawfulness of Muslims' buying and selling non-Muslims from hostile lands who had sold themselves and/or their children into slavery. However, to what extent can a reasonable person apply that issue to the countries targeted by Daesh today, where slavery is illegal, and where Muslims are free to practise their faith, building – or even converting disused church buildings into – mosques (see *Sahih al-Bukhari*, no.610); and where they carry Arabic copies of the Qur'an and may occasionally be seen in high streets of cities offering translations of the Qur'an to passers-by (see *Sahih Muslim*, no.1869b)?

Concerning the Muslims who enter *Darul Harb*, likewise if he kidnaps them or their children, or subdues them in any way, then the life and wealth of the *harbi kuffar* are permissible for the Muslim, so if they seize them in a *shar'i* manner, they own them.[25]

The scholars have only argued over the issue of when the disbeliever is guaranteed protection, does a Muslim have the right to buy their children from them? According to two statements in the schools of Abu Hanifah and Malik, and of Ahmad in one narration, it is permissible to buy their children from them. Indeed, Abu Hanifah and, in a recorded narration from him, Ahmad said that if the Muslims enter into a truce with the people of a country, and someone who took them captive sold them to the Muslims, it would be permissible to buy them from him. Malik and al-Shafi'i in another narration, however, took an opposing stance on that issue. Similarly, if some of the people of the land of war subdued, gifted or sold others, or some of them stole and sold or gifted others to the Muslims, you would be allowed to take possession of them just as Muslims would own them if they took possession of them by conquest.

25 Or, "Likewise, if he were to steal their persons or their children or to subdue them by some or other means – since the lives and property of enemy disbelievers are permissible to Muslims – if they take possession over them by legal means, they own them." This is the meaning of the Arabic text. However, as clear from the question that follows, this should not be considered Ibn Taymiyah's definitive opinion so much as his summarising of a legal problem of his day before outlining the conclusions of other scholars.

Soundbite 5: "*Kufr* alongside *muharabah* is present in every *kafir*..."

IBN TAYMIYAH (R) SAID, "KUFR ALONGSIDE MUHARABAH IS PRESENT IN EVERY KAFIR, SO IT IS PERMITTED TO ENSLAVE HIM, AS IT IS PERMITTED TO KILL HIM." -MAJMU ALFATAWA[26]

C5/1 The Sheikh – Allah have mercy on him – was asked about a Qurashi[27] man who married a female slave, who bore him a child. Is the child free or a slave?

C5/2 He responded: Praise be to Allah, Lord of the worlds. When a man marries a woman, knowing that she is a slave, then any child of hers from him is also a slave, by agreement of the leaders of the schools of law, for a child follows its father in lineage and filial duty, but follows its mother in terms of freedom or enslavement. If the child is from an ethnicity that may by general agreement be enslaved, then he is by general agreement a slave. However, if it is from an ethnicity over the enslavement of whom jurists disagree, then disagreement has occurred regarding the enslavement of Arabs. The correct stance is that the enslavement of both Arabs and non-Arabs is allowed based on what is established in the two *Sahih* collections, reported from Abu Hurayrah – Allah be pleased with him – who said, "I don't cease to love Banu Tamim after three things that I heard from Allah's Messenger PBUH say about them: [1] I heard Allah's Messenger PBUH say, 'They are the strongest of my *Ummah* against the Antichrist'; [2] when their zakat was brought, the Prophet PBUH said, 'This is the zakat of our people'; and [3] 'A'ishah had a slave girl from them, and the Prophet PBUH said, 'Free her, for she is a child of Ishmael'." And in Muslim's narration: "There are three traits that I heard from Allah's Messenger PBUH about Banu Tamim that have made me love them ever since: 'A'ishah had a freed slave, and Allah's Messenger PBUH told her, 'Free from these.' When their zakat came, he said, 'This is the zakat of my people.' He also said, 'They are the strongest of people when it comes to slaying in bloody battles.'"

---

26 See https://shamela.ws/book/7289/15596 (viewed 29/04/2025) for Arabic text of Ibn Taymiyah's response to *wa-su'ila al-shaykh rahimahu Allah 'an rajul Qurashi tazawwaja bi-jariyah mamlukah*.

27 The issue of the man's ethnic heritage is key here, as the Prophet PBUH was an Arab of the tribe of Quraysh, and he stated that his caliphs, or successors, should also be of that tribe.

C5/3 In the two *Sahih* collections, according to the wording in *Sahih Muslim*, from Abu Ayyub al-Ansari, the Prophet PBUH said, "Whoever says 'There is no God but Allah alone, with no partner, to Whom belongs dominion and praise, and Who has power over everything' ten times, he will be like the person who frees four people from the children of Ishmael." And there is mention in this hadith of the children of Ishmael being freed, which points to the fact of their enslavement, just as his PBUH enjoining 'A'ishah to free from the ethnicity of the freed slave, who was from the children of Ishmael, including Banu Tamim. Also in *Sahih al-Bukhari*, it is narrated from Marwan ibn al-Hakam and al-Miswar ibn Makhramah that, when the delegation from the Hawazin tribe came to Allah's Messenger PBUH as Muslims and asked him for their property and captives to be returned,[28] the Prophet PBUH stood up and told them, "I have with me those whom you see. The best of speech to me is that which is most truthful. So, choose one of the two alternatives, either the property or the captives, because I have been waiting for you." Allah's Messenger PBUH had waited for them some ten nights after returning from Taif. When it became clear to them that Allah's Messenger PBUH would only give them back one of the two alternatives, they said, "We choose our captives." So, Allah's Messenger PBUH stood amongst the Muslims, praised Allah as is His due, and then said, "To continue... You brothers have come to us in penitence. I have seen fit to return their captives to them. Whoever amongst you wishes generously to consent to that, let him do so; and whoever amongst you wishes to retain his share until we can give him from the first of whatever spoils Allah grants us, let him do so." The people present replied, "We have consented to that, O Messenger of Allah." So, Allah's Messenger PBUH said, "We do not know who has and who hasn't agreed to that, so go back and let the notables amongst you bring your decision to us." The people went back, and their notables spoke to them; then they returned to Allah's Messenger PBUH and informed him that they had given consent to acting generously. This authentic hadith relates to the captive womenfolk of Hawazin, who are Arabs, and whom he PBUH had

28 This account refers to an incident after the Prophet's PBUH victory at the Battle of Hunayn in 8/630, when he waited for the formal surrender of the Hawazin tribe, in order to give them a chance to choose before he distributed the spoils of war amongst the Muslims.

distributed amongst the victors, meaning that they had become their slaves. Thereafter he PBUH asked to take them from the Muslims either voluntarily or in return for compensation. The hadith mentions that he freed them, as occurred in the hadith of 'Umar, when he was on a religious retreat, and the news reached him that the Prophet PBUH had freed a captive, he too freed a slave woman whom he had. At that time, the Muslims would have sexual intercourse with such female captives by right of possession, as was the case with the captives of Awtas – namely, the captives of the Hawazin tribe – of whom the Prophet PBUH said, "Sexual intercourse is not to occur with a pregnant woman until she has given birth, nor one who is not pregnant until she is clear of her menstrual cycle."

C5/4 In *Musnad Ahmad*, it is narrated from 'A'ishah – Allah be pleased with her – who said, "Allah's Messenger PBUH divided the captives of Banu al-Mustaliq, and Juwayriyah bint al-Harith fell to the lot of Thabit ibn Qays ibn Shammas – or to one of his paternal uncles' sons – from whom she arranged to buy her freedom. She was an attractive, graceful woman. She came to Allah's Messenger PBUH and said, 'O Messenger of Allah, I am Juwayriyah bint al-Harith ibn Abi Dirar – of happy memory among his people – and I have suffered a calamity of which you are not unaware. I have come to you to seek your help in buying my freedom.' Allah's Messenger PBUH replied, 'Would you have something better than that?' She asked, 'What might that be, O Messenger of Allah?' He said, 'I pay for your freedom, and I marry you?' She responded, 'Yes, O Messenger of Allah!' He said, 'So be it.' The news got out to people that Allah's Messenger PBUH had married Juwayriyah bint al-Harith, so they set free what they possessed." 'A'ishah added, "So, by marrying her, he PBUH caused to be released a hundred household members from the Banu al-Mustaliq tribe. I know of no woman who brought more blessing to her people than her."

C5/5 These hadiths and others like them are famous; indeed, they reach the level of multiple narrations, that the Prophet PBUH would take captive slaves from among the Arabs, likewise the caliphs after him. As the four imams and others have said, "The Prophet PBUH would capture slaves from among the Arabs." Abu Bakr also captured slaves from Banu Najiyah and, by that enslavement, would deter the pagan Arabs from attacking. Allah told them (Q.4:24) *{and also forbidden to you are the chaste amongst married women, except those whom your right hands possess: Allah's decree upon you...}* that, in the hadith of Abu Sa'id and others, was revealed regarding captured female slaves, whom Allah permitted them to have sexual intercourse with through right of possession. If a woman is taken captive and enslaved without her husband, then sexual intercourse is permitted with her without doubt, though with one unusual dissenting opinion in the Hanbali school, the dissenting opinion being referred to by a scholar in the Maliki school. Ibn al-Mundhir said, "Everyone whose works are memorised from the people of knowledge is agreed that if a woman becomes someone's possession, and she has a husband resident in the land of war, her marriage to her husband becomes void, and sexual intercourse with her becomes lawful for the one who owns her after the completion of her menstrual cycle or pregnancy. However, if she is taken captive with her husband, there is disagreement amongst the people of knowledge. It is known that the type of enslavement that the Prophet PBUH practised generally happened in war. He fought the People of the Book. In the year of Tabuk, he left to fight the Christians, though no fighting took place; and he sent cavalry force against them, headed first by Zayd, then Ja'far, then 'Abd Allah ibn Rawahah, despite there being both Arabs and Byzantines among the Christians. Likewise, he fought the Jews at Khaybar, as well as the tribes of al-Nadir and Qaynuqa'; and among those Jews there were Arabs and Israelites. Similarly, the Jews of Yemen, among those Jews also there were Arabs* and Israelites. The reason for enslavement in such cases is disbelief, and conditional on the existence of a state of war. A free Muslim is not to be enslaved under any circumstances, nor is the non-Muslim with a covenant of protection or truce to be enslaved; but **every disbeliever in whom disbelief coexists with belligerence, enslaving him**

* In early seventh-century Yathrib, later Medina, the was a custom amongst Arabs, if a women suffered repeated miscarriages, to seek advice from their Jewish neighbours and to vow to raise any child born alive as a Jew (e.g. Sunan Abi Dawud, no.2682).

is permitted, just as fighting him is permitted.[29] Whatever makes the killing of combatants permissible makes permissible the enslavement of combatants' dependents; and this is a general rule regarding Arabs and non-Arabs, and this is the teaching of the Maliki school, of al-Shafi'i in the more recent of his two statements, and of Ahmad. As for Abu Hanifah, he does not allow the enslavement of Arabs, just as he does not allow charging them the *jizyah*[30] tax because, he argued, the Arabs were unique by virtue of their lineage, the Prophet PBUH being from them; and the disbelievers amongst them were unique in their excess of hostility towards him PBUH, so that became a constraint on accepting the *jizyah* from them just as, out of harshness towards them, the *jizyah* is not taken from apostates. And the last of Abu Hanifah's reasons is because of what occurred to himself[31] in terms of the honour of precedence in Islam; and he also quoted in evidence what has been narrated from 'Umar, that he said, "There is no taking ownership of an Arab…"[32] Those who have argued against Abu Hanifah have two statements on the permissibility of enslaving those from whom *jizyah* is not accepted, and both are narrated from Ahmad.

C5/6 One of the statements is that enslavement is like the charging of *jizyah*. So, whoever is not charged *jizyah* is not to be enslaved; and this is the view of the school of Abu Hanifah and others; and it is the chosen stance of al-Khiraqi, al-Qadi, and others of Ahmad's followers; and it is the

29 See https://shamela.ws/book/7289/15600 (viewed 29/04/2025) for Arabic text of *wa-al-kufr ma'a al-muharabah mawjud fi kull kafir fa-jaza istirqaquhu kama yajuzu qitaluhu*. The Daesh propagandists' translation ("Kufr alongside muharabah is present in every kafir, so it is permitted to enslave him, as it is permitted to kill him") is only possible linguistically when that one sentence is taken out of context. Here Ibn Taymiyah is presenting the differing opinions of earlier scholars on the issue before reaching his own conclusion. Furthermore, the linking of disbelief to the existence of a state of war as a precondition to lawful enslavement tends to undermine the point that the Daesh propagandists seem to be seeking to make.

30 The *jizyah* is a form of annual poll tax or tribute that is mentioned in the Qur'an (Q.9:29), and which is paid by *dhimmis*, as the non-Muslim citizens of Muslim lands are called.

31 Abu Hanifah's grandfather is traditionally seen as a client of the Banu Taym Allah.

32 This is part of a tradition recorded by al-Bayhaqi in his *al-Sunan al-kubra*, the chain of transmission of which is truncated (*munqata'*). It is therefore weak and so cannot be used as a basis for binding legal rulings. Ibn Taymiyah indicates his awareness of this by writing "what has been narrated from 'Umar, that he said" instead of simply "what 'Umar said."

position of al-Istarkhi from al-Shafi'i's followers. According to Abu Hanifah, *jizyah* may be accepted from every disbeliever except the Arab associators; and that is also one of the narrations from Ahmad. This not allowing Arab associators to be enslaved is due to *jizyah* not being taken from them, whereas non-Arab associators may be enslaved; and that is the statement of al-Shafi'i based on his other statement that Arabs are not enslaved. The other narration from Ahmad is that *jizyah* is only accepted from People of the Book and Zoroastrians, as with al-Shafi'i's school. Based on this statement in Ahmed's school, it is not permissible to enslave anyone from the associators, be they Arab or otherwise, which is the preferred opinion of al-Khiraqi, al-Qadi, and others. These two statements in the school of Ahmad do not prevent enslavement because of lineage but because of religion. So, if a Muslim soldier captures a pagan Arab woman, and she accepts Islam, he may enslave her; but if she does not willingly accept Islam, he should force her to accept it. They base this on what the Prophet PBUH and the companions used to do when enslaving Arabs. As for the male pagan slave,[33] according to those scholars, a fixed slave status for him is not permitted, as is permitted with *jizyah*. This is as when the companions took Arab and pagan women captive and had sexual intercourse with them, and the Prophet PBUH said, "Sexual intercourse is not to occur with a pregnant woman until she has given birth, nor one who is not pregnant until she is clear of her menstrual cycle." Thereafter the four imams have agreed that sexual intercourse should only be after a female slave's acceptance of Islam, and that sexual intercourse with a pagan slave woman is not permitted, just as marrying her is not permitted.

C5/7 The second statement against Abu Hanifah's view is that it is permitted to enslave those from the people of the idolatry from whom *jizyah* may not be taken. That is the view of al-Shafi'i's school and the latter narration of Ahmad, based on the fact that companions enslaved them, and that we do not know that they forced them to accept Islam. Also because,

33 Here the text uses the masculine as opposed to feminine, so Ibn Taymiyah is presumably intending a distinction to be drawn.

since it is not permitted to kill them, they must obviously be enslaved;[34] and slavery is – if anything – more demeaning than the taking of *jizyah*.

C5/8 It has become clear from what we have mentioned that the correct view is that the enslavement of Arabs is permissible. As for the tradition mentioned as from 'Umar, if it is authentic and clearly related to this dispute, Abu Bakr and 'Ali opposed it, since they did take Arabs captive. It may be that 'Umar's statement is related to Arabs who accepted Islam before their menfolk could be enslaved, so slavery was not imposed on them, as in the case of Quraysh, who accepted Islam *en masse*, hence slavery was not imposed on them on account of their accepting Islam, not on account of their lineage. Nor were the companions able to take the womenfolk of Quraysh captive as they were able to take the womenfolk of other Arab tribes captive, and for this reason, none of them was enslaved. Nothing prohibiting their being taken captive has been preserved from the Prophet PBUH. As for when an Arab marries a slave woman, the marriage of a free man to a slave woman is not allowed except if two conditions are met: [1] fear of sexual distress; and [2] lack of means to marry a free woman, according to the schools of Malik, al-Shafi'i, and Ahmad ibn Hanbal. They reached that conclusion because such a marriage would lead to the enslavement of his child. So, it is not permitted for a free man, Arab or non-Arab, to marry a slave woman except out of necessity; and if he marries her out of necessity, his child will be a slave. The constraint according to Abu Hanifah is that a free woman should be his wife; and he, of course, differentiates between the enslavement of Arabs and others. As for him having sexual intercourse with a slave woman by fornication, then her child would, by general scholarly agreement, be a slave of her owner, even if his father were an Arab, because lineage is unconnected. However, if he has sexual intercourse with her within marriage, thinking her to be free, or that he had sought to make sure that she was not pregnant and then had sexual

34 The opinion summarised here by Ibn Taymiyah is saying the opposite of what the above decontextualised Daesh quotation ("*Kufr alongside muharabah is present in every kafir, so it is permitted to enslave him, as it is permitted to kill him*") asserts, namely that, once any fighting has ended, it is not allowed to kill even a hostile male disbeliever in cold blood.

intercourse, imagining her to be his slave, here his child would be free regardless of whether he was an Arab or not. This man is termed 'deceived',[35] and the child of a deceived man, whether by marriage or sale, is free due to the man's belief that he had sexual intercourse with a wife who was free or owned respectively, and he must pay compensation to the slave woman's owner, as the companions ruled on that issue, because he deprived the slave woman's owner of ownership of her and any children, liability for which is on him. On that last point, there are ramifications and disputes that this is not the place to outline.[36] And Allah knows best.

35 Ibn Taymiyah here uses the word 'deceived' (*maghrur*) as a legal term, coined by jurists presumably out of necessity due to the opportunity that slavery gave to the unscrupulous to dupe men into sexual intercourse with a woman whose true social status was concealed at the time of the marriage or sale, which could be seen as a form of prostitution, which is recognised in the Qur'an as existing and is obviously prohibited (Q.24:33).

36 What Ibn Taymiyah describes here regarding the status of children born of enslaved women and free men is analogous to the legal doctrine of *partus sequitur ventrem* in colonial and post-independence America until slavery was finally abolished there in 1865.

Soundbite 6: "It is allowed for the Muslim who enters *Darul Harb*..."

SHAWKANI (R) SAID, "IT IS ALLOWED FOR THE MUSLIM WHO ENTERS DARUL HARB (WITH AN AMAN FROM ITS PEOPLE) TO TAKE WHATEVER HE IS ABLE OF THEIR WEALTH & TO SHED WHATEVER HE IS ABLE TO OF THEIR BLOOD."-ASSAYLAL JARRAÃR[37]

C6/1 Commentary on al-Mahdi li-Din Allah's statement in *al-Azhar*][38], "Section: And the land of war is a land of permissibility," etc., I say that the sense of this is that Allah – may He be glorified – commanded us to fight the people of idolatry, and He permitted us to shed their blood, and to seize their wealth and women. From this standpoint, on the principle of permissibility, the disbelievers remain, regardless of whether we find them in their land or some other land. So, it is proper to restrict this generalisation, since the sanctity of a Muslim's life and his wealth persists, whichever land he is in. Hence it is not permissible for any Muslim to violate that sanctity on the grounds that "the land of war is a land of permissibility." Rather it should be seen from that standpoint that we have already mentioned, in other words, not absolute. Indeed, the author himself pointed this out in his statement "except for a free person who has accepted Islam..." As for allowing the sale of whatever has been taken from the land of war from whoever has it in possession, that is the apparent meaning because the taker owns what he has taken possession of. However, if the taker is a Muslim, then his statement "even a father from a son" is invalid because a Muslim is called on to follow the rulings of Islam in their entirety, including the obligation to free his kin; whereas if the seller is a disbeliever, then there is no problem in principle with buying his kin from him because, even if he claims its

37 See https://shamela.ws/book/7342/1048 (viewed 29/04/2025) for the Arabic text of *Qawluhu fasl wa-dar al-harb dar ibahah*.

38 Muhammad ibn 'Ali al-Shawkani (d.1250/1839) was a Yemeni scholar, born into a Zaydi family, who chose instead to adopt a holistic Sunni stance, in which he excelled. He is considered by some to be a forerunner of what is today called 'Salafism'. He composed this commentary not so much to explain as to point out the inadequacies of the well-established manual of Zaydi law, *al-Azhar fi fiqh al-a'immah al-athar* by Ahmad ibn Yahya, known as al-Mahdi li-Din Allah (d.840/1437). In this excerpt from al-Shawkani's *al-Sayl al-jarrar al-mutadaffiq 'alá hada'iq al-Azhar*, the original text from *al-Azhar* appears "between inverted commas" in the translation.

legality, any neglect in acting on what is legal is considered his sin. As for a Muslim's accepting from him the validity of his claim of legality, where the seller is a disbeliever, then no, because Islam is a precondition.[39]

C6/2 As for his statement "even if he has turned apostate," his intention is what preceded it that apostates should not be enslaved but asked to accept Islam again. If he does so, so be it; but if not, he should be killed.

C6/3 Regarding his statement "There is no retribution at all in the land of war," I say that this has no basis either in scripture or in tradition or, indeed, in sound analogy or consensus. The rulings of the law are binding on Muslims wherever they may be, and the land of war does not abrogate legal rulings in their entirety, or even some of them. What Allah required of Muslims in terms of retribution is fixed in the land of war just as it is fixed elsewhere, whatever loophole we may find to that. Nor is there any difference between retribution and the immutability of blood money except as an illusion that vanishes into thin air. Both of them are an inalienable human right, a ruling on which must be settled against his opponent; and he has the authority to choose which of the two to apply. The aim of what has been established regarding this is what occurred in relation to him PBUH in setting aside the blood feuds dating back to the days of the Age of Ignorance. There is no contradiction in this relating to the shedding of Muslim blood, which is based on what appears in the laws of Islam. The only thing that can suspend any of these laws is evidence that warrants being reported.[40] If there is none, then one must

39 In other words, what al-Shawkani seems to be saying is that a Muslim cannot accept the validity of a trade on the strength of a disbeliever's claim about the legality of the sale under his own code of practice, since compliance with both the spirit and letter of the Sharia is a precondition on validity for Muslims; and kindness to parents is a requirement in Islam. To take another example, according to Ibn Qudamah in *al-Mughni*, because a Muslim is bound by God's law, he cannot lawfully enter into, and profit from, a trade with a disbeliever that involves usury (see para. A1/7 in the appendix below). Even if it is the disbeliever who suggests such usurious terms to the benefit of the Muslim and declares himself content to proceed, the Muslim must not agree to them because, at the same time as pronouncing commerce lawful, God has forbidden usury outright (Q.2:275).

40 i.e. sound evidence from the Qur'an or the Sunnah. The point being made is that the Prophet's PBUH decision to set aside outstanding retribution for any blood that was shed during the Age of Ignorance before Islam became established in Medina was to spare his followers from perpetuating, as Muslims, vendettas from before they had accepted Islam. It did not mean that the blood that

remain with what is established in law on applying the requirement of both retribution and blood money.

C6/4 Regarding his statement "Their guarantee of safety to a Muslim implies a reciprocal guarantee of safety to them from him," I say there is no inherent legal, rational or customary link between these two guarantees of safety. *It is allowed for the Muslim who enters Darul Harb (with an aman from its people) to take whatever he is able of their wealth and to shed whatever he is able to of their blood.*[41] So, his statement does not follow logically that "He should not plunder their goods," nor his statement "and he should return whatever he has bought from someone who has plundered them after the guarantee of safety."

C6/5 As for his statement "He should not approve any invalid condition,"[42] etc., its intended purpose is clear, since this guarantee of safety is tantamount to compromising over the allotted time of his death. It is not permitted to enter into a pact which makes what is lawful unlawful or which makes what is unlawful lawful, as appears in authentic evidence. Likewise, what is invalid is invalid by legal ruling. How then is permissible for the disbelievers to impose an invalid condition, let alone its being permissible for them to approve it?

---

some of them had shed in the past, as disbelievers, was insignificant, but that reconciling past warring tribes was even more important.

41 Or, "It is permissible for a Muslim who has entered the land of war with a guarantee of safety from its people to take whatever wealth of theirs he can, shed whatever blood of theirs he can." See https://shamela.ws/book/7342/1049 (viewed 29/04/2025) for the Arabic text of *fa-yajuzu lil-Muslim al-dakhil dar al-harb bi-aman ahliha*. The point al-Shawkani is seeking to make here is that mere acceptance of a guarantee of safety from hostile non-Muslims does not necessitate reciprocation on the Muslim's part. This seems contrary to what Ibn Qudamah, for example, wrote in *al-Mughni* (see para. A1/7 in the appendix below): "[...] they have granted him safety conditional on his desisting from cheating them and on keeping them safe from himself. Even if it is not mentioned verbally, nevertheless its meaning is understood as implied."

42 For comparison, see the *Code of Conduct for members of the Armed Forces of the United States*. Article iii, "If I am captured, I will continue to resist by all means available. I will make every effort to escape and aid others to escape. I will accept neither parole nor special favors from the enemy." This code of conduct was issued by President Eisenhower with Executive Order 10631 in 1955, as a result of experiences during the Korean War.

C6/6 As for his statement "He may seek the return of a runaway slave," we have already mentioned that it is permissible for a Muslim to take whatever wealth of theirs he can. So, the fact that a Muslim is permitted to seize his runaway slave is obvious from the underlying sense of the text.

C6/7 As for his statement "Whoever has no guarantee of safety may take whatever he seizes," it is superfluous based on what preceded it, namely that, in terms of the disbelievers, he may plunder their lives and property, not to mention his statement at the beginning of this section, "And the land of war is a land of permissibility."

C6/8 As for his statement "and he is not required to pay a fifth," it cannot have escaped you that if the author had been completely honest about whatever was taken being booty, then it would have come under the terms of His words (Q.8:41) *{and know that whatever booty you seize}*[43] So, it is necessary to produce evidence specific to this version of the facts in the text, but there is no evidence.[44]

---

43 This verse (Q.8:41), which al-Shawkani assumes his readers will know in full, continues *{and know that whatever booty you seize, a fifth of it belongs to Allah and to the Messenger and his relatives, to orphans, the needy and the traveller, if you believe in Allah and in what We revealed to Our servant on the day of separating truth from falsehood, when the two armies met. Allah has power over all things.}*

44 Al-Shawkani's commentary appears to be highlighting a lack of logic in the Zaydi book *al-Azhar* in that if plundering from non-Muslims is permitted because a particular place is a land of war, then a fifth of its value must be deducted in accordance with the Qur'an injunction on booty. Taking booty is different from theft, which is both a sin and a crime.

Soundbite 7: "& if a people in Darul Harb embrace Islam..."

SAHNUN (R) SAID, "& IF A PEOPLE IN DARUL HARB EMBRACE ISLAM, IT IS PERMISSIBLE FOR THEM TO KILL WHOEVER THEY CAN & TAKE THEIR WEALTH."-AN NAWADIR WA-ZIYADAT[45]

C7/1 Regarding a Muslim prisoner of war or whoever accepts Islam in the land of war, does he have the right to do whatever he can in terms of escaping, criminality, killing or taking captives? What about if they release him conditionally, or he gives them is word over certain matters? And what about if he fornicates or steals?

C7/2 From Ibn al-Mawaz's[46] book, and it is also in *al-'Utbiyah*,[47] reported from Asbagh and from Ibn al-Qasim, who said about the Muslim prisoner of war, if he is able to escape[48] from whoever of the enemy has him, either he is left to come and go as he pleases, in which case it is permissible for him to flee unless he is released on parole.[49] If his being left to come and go has no parole condition, then **he may kill, plunder and take whatever**

45 See https://shamela.ws/book/96257/1470 (viewed 01/05/2025) for the Arabic text of *Fi al-asir al-Muslim aw man aslama bi-dar al-harb*. The work's full title work is *al-Nawadir wa-al-ziyadat 'ala ma fi al-Mudawwanah min ghayriha min al-ummahat* by Abu Muhammad 'Abd Allah ibn 'Abd al-Rahman Abi Zayd al-Qayrawani (d.386/996). The title of the book from which this excerpt is taken refers to those unusual opinions not found in *al-Mudawwanah* but only other core Maliki texts.

46 Muhammad ibn Ibrahim, known as Ibn al-Mawaz (d.269/882 or 3), wrote a book on Maliki law called *al-Mawaziyah*. The opinions in this book may therefore be taken as 'exploratory' rather than of acknowledged authority within the Maliki school.

47 This refers to the work of Muhammad ibn Ahmad al-'Utbi (d.255/869)

48 See also the footnote to C6/5 above on Article iii of the *Code of Conduct for members of the Armed Forces of the United States*, "If I am captured, I will continue to resist by all means available. [...] I will accept neither parole nor special favors from the enemy."

49 Compare Article 21 of the *Geneva Convention relative to the Treatment of Prisoners of War* states that "Prisoners of war may be partially or wholly released on parole or promise, insofar as is allowed by the laws of the Power on which they depend. Such measures shall be taken particularly in cases where this may contribute to the improvement of their state of health. No prisoner of war shall be compelled to accept liberty on parole or promise. [...] Prisoners of war who are paroled or who have given their promise in conformity with the laws and regulations so notified, are bound on their personal honour scrupulously to fulfil, both towards the Power on which they depend and towards the Power which has captured them, the engagements of their paroles or promises."

he can;[50] likewise anyone of them who was held under restraint but managed to break his bonds by himself. Either that, or he is released from restraint on condition that he does not attempt to escape or to act treacherously towards them; such a person does not have the leeway to do that.

C7/3 'Isa narrated something similar from Ibn al-Qasim,[51] who said, "Someone of whom I approve said it"[52] – and I suspect that it was Malik who said it – "of a prisoner of war who, on a guarantee of safety, is not restrained, he is not permitted to escape or to take anything of theirs. However, if they release him without any guarantee of safety, as they might release a slave, and they show no fear of him, then he has the right to escape and take what he can."

C7/4 Ibn al-Mawaz said, "Except where those who released him from his bonds left him in a place from which he cannot escape, leaving him on the basis that he would not escape, this person has the right to make what he can of that situation."

C7/5 Ibn al-Mawaz also said, "Ibn al-Qasim said, 'If they did not impose that condition on him at the time of releasing him from his bonds, then he

---

50 This is closest text found to the Daesh quotation, *"& if a people in Darul Harb embrace Islam, it is permissible for them to kill whoever they can and take their wealth."* The assertion in the Daesh soundbite that a person who converts to Islam in 'the land of war' can plunder and kill as much as he is able appears to have no basis except in the question, since the opinion in the response itself refers only to Muslim prisoners of war who were not released conditionally on parole.

51 'Abd al-Rahman ibn al-Qasim (d.191/806) studied for about twenty years under Malik ibn Anas, the founder of the Maliki school of jurisprudence.

52 This peculiar turn of phrase ("Someone of whom I approve said it...") appears in a number of Maliki law books, but not readily in the works of Hanafi, Shafi'i or Hanbali scholars. Sahnun (d.240/854), who studied under students of Imam Malik ibn Anas, is mentioned in the soundbite as given to me by a convicted terrorist, but not in the quotation itself. In this instance, Sahnun rather than Malik may or may not have been the person approved of by Ibn al-Qasim. However, why would Ibn al-Qasim refer to his own student, Sahnun, in this way rather than just naming his source for this opinion along lines that – out of context – appears to support Daesh propaganda? Either way, whatever one thinks of the opinion, it would have been clear to the originally intended readership with legal training that, under the normal rules of engagement, an escaped PoW would only be allowed to attack and kill those who presented a clear threat to their own safety and survival.

has the right to do whatever he can in terms of seizing property, killing, and taking women and children captive. However, if he is released on condition that he does not try to escape or to engage in any unlawful act, then he is not permitted to do any of that, as in the case of a compact."[53]

---

53 This clear statement is particularly relevant when one thinks of the serious incident at the separation centre in HMP Frankland on Saturday 12th April 2025, when Hashem Abedi assaulted three prison officers with hot butter or cooking oil and improvised bladed weapons, apparently made from a baking tray. Before using kitchen facilities or gym equipment, prisoners must sign a compact undertaking to do so in a safe manner. As we read in the excerpt above, which is only included here because Daesh propagandists chose to misquote it, such a compact is considered legally binding from the Sharia perspective, even if a Muslim considers him- or herself to be not a criminal, but a prisoner of war. Whilst knowledge of this fact may not have dissuaded Hashem Abedi from acting as he did on that day, it is not unreasonable to assume that it might be helpful in giving the majority of Muslim prisoners the confidence to view such assaults as contrary to the teachings of Islam rather than as heroic acts of jihad against oppression by the *kuffar* (disbelievers).

Soundbite 8: "There is no *qisas* for the one who kills a *harbi kafir*..."

IBN QUDAMAH (R) SAID, "THERE IS NO QISAS FOR THE ONE WHO KILLS A HARBI KAFIR, DUE TO THE STATEMENT OF ALLAH, {THEN KILL THE POLYTHEISTS WHEREVER YOU FIND THEM}, NOR FOR THE ONE WHO KILLS A MURTAD & BECAUSE HE IS ONE WHOSE BLOOD IS PERMISSIBLE TO BE SHED, HE IS MORE RESEMBLING OF THE HARBI KAFIR." -AL KAFI FI FIQH AL-IMAM AHMED[54]

C8/1 Section: *There is no qisas for the one who kills a harbi kafir, due to the statement of Allah, {Then kill the polytheists wherever you find them}, nor for the one who kills a murtad and because he is one whose blood is permissible to be shed, he is more resembling of the harbi kafir,* [55] nor, likewise, against the killer of an adulterer, regardless of whether the killer is Muslim or a protected person. If he kills someone whom he recognises as an apostate who had subsequently accepted Islam again, but he did not know of his acceptance of Islam, there are two opinions, the first of which is that there is no retribution against him because he didn't aim to kill an innocent, so he is not bound by retribution just as if, in the land of war, he had killed someone whom he thought was a hostile non-Muslim after he had accepted Islam. The second opinion is that there is retribution against him because he killed someone of equivalent religious and social standing as himself out of deliberate hostility. The apparent sense is that he is not exempt in the land of Islam, unless it be after the victim has accepted Islam, as opposed to someone in the land of war. If he kills someone whom he recognises as protected by covenant or a slave, and he himself had accepted Islam and been freed from slavery, then there is retribution against him because he intended to kill an innocent, who was of equivalent standing to himself, so like someone who knows his condition.

54 See https://shamela.ws/book/21731/1144 (viewed 01/05/2025) for the Arabic text of *Fasl wa-la qisas 'ala qatil harbi*.

55 Or, "And there is no retribution against the killer of a hostile associator due to Allah the Exalted's words (Q.9:5) *{so, slay the associators wherever you find them}* nor, likewise, against the killer of an apostate, since shedding his blood is permitted similarly to the hostile associator."

Soundbite 9: "Allah made the blood and wealth of the *kafir* lawful..."

IMAM SHAAFI (R) SAID, "ALLAH MADE THE BLOOD & WEALTH OF THE KAFIR LAWFUL UNLESS HE PAYS THE JIZYA OR IS GIVEN A COVENANT OF SECURITY FOR A PERIOD OF TIME."-AL UMM[56]

C9/1 Al-Shafi'i[57] – may Allah have mercy upon him – said: Some people have said that if a woman reverts to disbelief from Islam, she should be held in captivity and not killed. To whoever makes this statement, I have asked, "Have you said this based on a sound report or on analogical reasoning?" He has replied, "Rather on a report from Ibn 'Abbas, who was one of the best of the people of knowledge from those of his viewpoint, so it is said," I responded, "Whoever has said that is wrong, and amongst them are those who utter more such idle claims." And I said to him, "Some of your hadith scholars have narrated from Abu Bakr that he had women who reverted from Islam killed. It is therefore not right for us to use this as evidence, as it is considered weak by those knowledgeable in the science of hadiths." He replied, "Then I am saying it by way of analogy with the Sunnah." I said, "So, mention it." He replied, "Allah's Messenger PBUH forbade the killing of women and children from the people the land of war. So, if the womenfolk of the people of the land of war are not to be killed, then precedence should be given surely to not killing those women whose immunity due to acceptance of Islam has been established."

C9/2 I, al-Shafi'i, asked the other person, "Does the ruling for the land of war resemble the ruling for the land of Islam?" He responded, "What's the difference between them?" I said, "You differentiate between them." "Where?" he asked. I replied, "Consider the frail old man, the monk, the hired labourer. Should any of those be killed in the land of war?" He said, "No!" "What then if a Muslim man reverts to disbelief and becomes a

56 See https://shamela.ws/book/1655/283 (viewed 02/05/2025) for the Arabic text of *Qala al-Shafi'i rahimahu Allah ta 'ala qala ba'd al-nas idha artaddat al-mar'ah 'an al-Islam*.

57 In the printed edition, this section has the heading *al-Khilaf fi al-murtadd* (*The dispute over the apostate*). Without going any further, what is clear is that the soundbite on the lawfulness or otherwise of slaying disbelievers, which has been extracted from this legal opinion, does not relate to the main issue under consideration by al-Shafi'i. Rather it must be deemed a peripheral matter to the issue of adult female apostasy.

monk," I said, "or a Muslim hired labourer reverts to disbelief, should we kill him?" "Yes!" he replied. "Why," I ask, "when these were of those whose immunity due to acceptance of Islam had been established, but they then become disbelievers, why is their blood not spared?" "Because," he answered, "the killing of these apostates is like a prescribed penalty, and I have no right to suspend it."

C9/3 I asked, "Do you think regarding what you have just ruled in the case of a prescribed penalty, should we let it lapse in the case of a woman? Thinking about killing, amputation, stoning or flogging, do you find any difference between Muslim men and women regarding this?" "No!" he said. So, I said, "Why would you not have her killed in accordance with the prescribed penalty for apostasy?" and I, al-Shafi'i, added, "Do you agree that the property of a woman from the land of war can be plundered and that she may be taken captive and enslaved?" "Yes!" he replied. "So," I asked, "would you do that with a female apostate in the land of Islam?" "No!" he replied. So, I asked him, "How are you permitted to draw a comparison between one thing and another that is dissimilar in both cases?"

C9/4 al-Shafi'i went on to say, "Some people say, 'If a man reverts from Islam to disbelief and is killed or dies as an apostate, or he reaches the land of war, we divide his estate amongst his Muslim heirs; we settle every debt against him for a period; we manumit the mothers of his children and those of his slaves to whom he promised freedom after his death. If thereafter he returns to Islam, we do not revoke any of that ruling unless we find some of his property still in the hands of any of his heirs, and they return it to him because it is his property; and whichever of his heirs expends any of what we gave him of the former apostate's wealth by way of inheritance, he is not answerable for that." I, al-Shafi'i, said to the most respected amongst those who said that, "According to you, knowledge is based on four core principles, the foremost and most necessary of which to take from, not abandon, are the Book of Allah and the Sunnah of His Prophet PBUH. However, I know only that you have peeled away against both of these, then leaving only analogy and, according to you, the rational next principle to take from after those two is consensus; and yet you have gone against analogy and reason, instead saying something contradictory." He responded, "So show me what you have thus described." I told him, "Blessed and Exalted Allah said (Q.4:176) *{If a man perishes, having no child, but having a sister, then half of what he leaves behind is hers; and he shall inherit from her, if she had no child.}* along with whatever else He mentioned in the verses on inheritance. Do you not see that Majestic and Mighty Allah only gave the living possession of the inheritance that the deceased owned when they were alive?" "Of course!" he said. "And," I continued, "are not the living different from the dead?" "Yes!" he replied. "So, what do you think then," I asked, "of the apostate who, passing through some of our frontier posts, joins a camp he sees of the people of war, ready to fight us, or to become a monk, or just to isolate himself, so that nothing is known of his life? How do you apply against him a ruling relating to the dead when he is still alive? Did you say that on the basis of a report or by analogy?" He said, "I said it on the basis of a report." I said, "Then how did you miss that the Leader of the Faithful, 'Umar ibn al-Khattab, and 'Uthman ibn 'Affan too, ruled regarding the wife of a missing person to hold on four years and then observe the prescribed waiting period; and that they made no ruling regarding his property?" Then I added, "Glory be to Allah! Is it permissible to issue a ruling relating to those deceased against his estate, even if the likelihood is that he is dead, because he may not be dead, and a ruling on him should not be issued except on the basis of certainty? You, however, have on the same day issued a ruling as if he were deceased regarding the disposal of everything, based on your opinion, then you have made a contradictory statement." He responded, "Have you not considered that I may have seized the apostate and then slain him?" I replied, "Perhaps you seize him but do not slay him as he is in a state of delirium or is mute when seized, so you'd have to wait until he came round in order to see if he'd repent." "Yes!" he said.

C9/5 So, I asked, "Have you considered if you were to slay him on seizing him, would that still necessitate a ruling as if he were deceased if you had neither seized nor slain him? Or perhaps you seize him but do not slay him because he repents after being seized or before becoming mute?" He replied, "In that case, I say that if he turns apostate and reaches the land of war, then the ruling on him is as if he were deceased." So, I said to him, "Is it permissible to say that a deceased person is alive without verifiable news of that? If this is permissible for you, the same is also permissible for others than you; then, by the same token, ignorant people would have the right to talk freely about what is lawful and unlawful." "They don't have that right," he said. "And whyever not?" I asked. "Because," he said, "it is for the people of knowledge alone to speak about what is lawful and unlawful on the basis of a Qur'anic scripture, prophetic injunction, consensus, tradition, analogy or reason, and not to talk on the basis of whatever else people may know unless some Qur'anic scripture, prophetic injunction, consensus or tradition, as it is not permitted to differ solely on the basis of analogy." Is this a prophetic injunction?" I asked. "Yes!" he replied. "Then," I said, "you have spoken contrary Qur'anic scripture, analogy and reason." "In what way have I contradicted analogy?" he asked. "Have you not considered," I responded, "when you claimed that if he turns apostate and reaches the land of war, you must issue a ruling as if he were deceased, yet you do not overturn the ruling if he comes back? This is because, once you have issued a ruling regarding him, it is binding on you. However, supposing a prophetic injunction were to come along,[58] so you leave him without ruling on his property for ten years until he comes back repentant. Then he on whom you had previously issued a ruling as if they were deceased requests that you surrender that property to him, saying, 'It is binding on you to give us this property back even after ten years.'" He said, "I wouldn't give it to them, and he has every right to his property." I replied to him, "What if they say, 'You are bound by this ruling, so it is unlawful for you not to give us that property.

58 Imam al-Shafi'i (d.204/820) died when al-Bukhari (d.256/870) was barely ten years old, and the same year as Muslim ibn al-Hajjaj (d.261/875) was born. So, he would have been fully aware that his knowledge of the Sunnah, though extensive, was incomplete. This is perhaps the basis for this comment, and for his saying that "If ever you find in my writings what contradicts the Sunnah of Allah's Messenger PBUH, go with the Sunnah of Allah's Messenger PBUH and abandon what I have said," taken from al-Nawawi's introduction to *al-Majmu' sharh al-Muhadhdhab*.

However, if you weren't bound to act except on his death, then you have given us his property in circumstances where it was lawful neither for you nor for us'?"

C9/6 I, al-Shafi'i, then said to him, "When you claimed that if you issue a ruling on him as if he were dead, did you consider the question 'What prevents the ruling on him being either enforceable and irrevocable or else suspended and revoked if he returns?' He said, "This isn't exactly what I'm saying." I said, "Do you then distinguish between it on the basis of information that is binding so that we may follow it?" He said, "No!" So, I said, "If the disagreement is between analogy and reason, and you make an assertion without a reliable report, is it permissible?" He replied, "It's only your companions who make a distinction without a reliable report." Do you consider that correct from those of them who do it?" I asked. "No!" he replied. "Or have you also considered," I asked, "in your opinion if he has a debt that is due in thirty years, and he reaches the land of war, so you settle the debt to the creditor to the value of one hundred thousand dinars, you free the slave mothers of his children and those other slaves whom he had declared would be free on his death, and you divide up his estate between his two sons, so that each one gets a thousand dinars, which one of the squanders and the other retains; then he comes back as a Muslim on the very same day or the next, and says, 'Give me back what is mine, namely this property and these slave mothers of my children and those other slaves, exactly as they were. Here's my creditor saying, "This is his money in possession, unaltered"; and here are my two sons, one of whom still has my money to hand, while the other is avoiding me, having squandered my wealth'?" He said, "I'd tell him, 'The ruling has been carried out, and it will not be overturned except that I will give you that which your son has in possession who didn't squander it.'" So I said to him, "What if he said to you, 'Why not repay me from another source?'" He replied, "Because it has to be your wealth exactly as it was." So, I said, "But the slaves promised freedom on his death, and the slave mothers of his children, and the deferred debt, they are all his wealth exactly as it was; so why not give it to him?" He replied, "I wouldn't give him it because the ruling has been carried out." I said, "But the ruling was carried out regarding what you gave his son."

He answered, “Yes!” I said, “So, you have issued a single ruling. If it is right to implement it, implement it in total; but it is right to overturn it, overturn it in total.” He replied, “I would return whatever wealth I found exactly as it was.” So, I said to him, “Then return to him his deferred debt exactly as it was, and the slaves promised freedom on his death, and the slave mothers of his children.” He responded, “I’d return exactly what I found in his heir’s possession.” I retorted, “Do you consider this an answer?” He added nothing except to say, “So, where is the prophetic injunction?” I, al-Shafi‘i, then said to him, “Malik informed us from Ibn Shihab, from ‘Ali ibn Husayn, from ‘Amr ibn ‘Uthman, from Usamah ibn Zayd that Allah’s Messenger PBUH said, ‘A Muslim does not inherit from a disbeliever.’” I, al-Shafi‘i, then said, “Sufyan informed us from al-Zuhri, from ‘Ali ibn Husayn, from ‘Amr ibn ‘Uthman, from Usamah ibn Zayd that Allah’s Messenger PBUH said similar to that.” I continued, “Is there any dispute over whether an apostate is a disbeliever or a Muslim?” He said, “Indeed, he is a disbeliever; and on that basis I would slay him.” I said, “Isn’t it clear to you that a Muslim should not inherit from a disbeliever?” He replied, “We have narrated from ‘Ali ibn Abi Talib – may Allah be pleased with him – that he had distributed the estate of an apostate whom he had executed to his Muslim heirs.”

C9/7 I, al-Shafi‘i, then said, “I’ve heard you and others claim that what has been narrated from ‘Ali about his distribution of the estate of an apostate is incorrect, and that the memorisers of the Sunnah don’t narrate within the Hadith corpus.” He replied, “Those who narrated it are trustworthy. We only say that it is wrong by inference, and that is speculation.” I then told him, “al-Thaqafi, who is trustworthy, narrated from Ja‘far ibn Muhammad, from his father – may Allah have mercy on them both – from Jabir that the Prophet PBUH gave judgement for a witness based on a solemn oath,” adding, “yet the memorisers of the Sunnah don’t mention Jabir, which implies that there is an error. Have you therefore considered if we were to argue against you using your same proof, saying, ‘This is speculation, but al-Thaqafi is trustworthy,’ even though what others have done is far closer to the truth?” He said, “In that case, you wouldn’t be entirely fair.” I responded, “Likewise, you weren’t being entirely fair when you informed me that the memorisers of the Sunnah narrated this hadith from 'Ali – may Allah be pleased with him. There's nothing in it about distributing his wealth." And I added, "This is incorrect, yet you argued on that basis." So, he said, "What if it is established practice?" I replied, "The principle that we go by, not just us but you and the people of knowledge, is whatever is established as coming from Allah's Messenger PBUH; and anything contrary established from others, no matter how many they are, is not a proof." He said, "True! However, I am saying that it is possible that the Prophet's PBUH statement, 'A Muslim does not inherit from a disbeliever,' refers to the disbeliever who has never entered Islam." I, al-Shafi'i, then said to him, "Are you saying that based on an indication in the hadith?" "No!" he replied, "But 'Ali – may Allah be pleased with him – knew better." So, I said, "Did 'Ali narrate this hadith from the Prophet PBUH, so that we could say that he left out nothing of what he narrated from the Prophet PBUH whose meaning he knew to indicate what you have said?" He replied, "I don't know of him narrating it from the Prophet PBUH." I asked, "Is it possible then that 'Ali didn't hear it?" "Yes!" he replied.

C9/8 I, al-Shafi'i, then said to him, "Do you still consider that you have some proof regarding this?" He said, "It's unlikely that something like this would be hidden from 'Ali – may Allah be pleased with him." So, I said, "I've also found you reporting that the Prophet PBUH adjudicated in the case of Birwa' bint Washiq, who had married without a dower, that she receive a dower similar to women of her status; yet 'Ali gave a contrary judgement, and I too have heard that." He said, "Like the statement of 'Ali ibn 'Umar, of Zayd ibn Thabit and of Ibn 'Abbas." So, I said, "No one nor his opinion constitutes a proof alongside the Sunnah of the Prophet PBUH." Then I told him, "If someone were to say to you, 'It may be that Zayd and Ibn 'Umar and Ibn 'Abbas only said this because they knew that the Prophet PBUH knew that the husband of Birwa' had specified an amount for her after contracting the marriage; so, on that basis, Ma'qil ibn Yasar al-Muzani committed to memory that contracting a marriage should come after settling the amount of the dower.' Yet these aforementioned companions knew that the amount fell due after consummation of a marriage." He responded, "It isn't mentioned in the Ma'qil hadith; and these narrators didn't narrate it or they would have said it in a narration. Rather, they only said 'We will go with this opinion,' until they produce a narration on this issue." So, I, al-Shafi'i, asked him, "Why has what you narrated from 'Ali about the apostate been treated thus?" I then said to him, "Mu'adh ibn Jabal used to rule that a Muslim could inherit from a disbeliever; likewise Mu'awiyah, Ibn al-Musayyib, Muhammad ibn 'Ali, and others. Some of them even said, 'We can inherit from them, but they don't inherit from us, just as their women[59] are lawful for us, whereas our women aren't lawful for them.' Have you considered if someone were to say, 'Mu'adh ibn Jabal is from the people of knowledge among the companions of Allah's Messenger PBUH, and Allah's Messenger's PBUH hadith may imply that "A Muslim does not inherit from a disbeliever" from among the idol-worshippers, because most of his PBUH rulings were against them. Their women are not lawful in marriage, but a Muslim can inherit from a disbeliever of the People of the Book just as marriage to one of their women is lawful.'" He replied, "That is not for that person to say. The hadith implies much of what has been laid on it, but Mu'adh isn't a proof even if he said something that the hadith implies, because he didn't narrate the hadith." I said, "So, we say to you, 'Suppose Mu'adh knows nothing of that, and it is Usamah ibn Zayd who narrated it.'" "Yes!" he said, "Someone more senior in companionship of the Prophet PBUH may be ignorant of a particular prophetic injunction whilst someone with relatively little companionship does know it."

C9/9 So, I, al-Shafi'i, asked him, "How is it that you didn't say this regarding the apostate issue?" Then al-Shafi'i noted that the other interrupted, saying, "And why did you say that the apostate's wealth becomes booty?" I replied, "Based on the fact that Allah – Blessed and Exalted be He – forbade shedding the blood and taking wealth of the believer except in one of the circumstances that makes it binding; but Allah made the blood and wealth of the kafir lawful unless he pays the *jizya* or is given a covenant of security for

59 Implied here, as becomes clear below, is that it is lawful in the Sharia for Muslim men to marry women of the People of the Book, but not *vice versa*.

a period of time.[60] That which renders shedding the blood of the adult male associator permissible is that the same as that which makes taking his wealth permissible; and that wealth is subject to Him Who is Mightier than wealth. So, when an apostate leaves Islam, he becomes one who fits the meaning of someone whose blood is permitted to be shed due to disbelief, not for any other reason, and the ruling on his wealth is pursuant to his blood. It should not be that, whilst the bond of Islam is dissolved so that shedding his blood is permissible, his wealth remains protected." Then, al-Shafi'i reported that the other said, "If you class him like the people of the land of war, then you have grouped them in one respect but separated them in another." "How so?" I asked. He replied, "You do not plunder his wealth until he has either died or you've slain him; whereas the wealth of the enemy disbeliever may be plundered before he either dies or is slain."

C9/10 So, I, al-Shafi'i, told him, "The ruling on the people of the land of war is twofold: (a) either the call to Islam has already reached him, in which case I would attack him without any further call to Islam and seize his wealth, even if I do not slay him; or (b) the call to Islam has not yet reached him, in which case I wouldn't attack him until I've called him to Islam; nor would I plunder his wealth until I've called him to Islam, and he refuses, making shedding his blood and taking his wealth lawful. However, when talking about an apostate, he should be called back to Islam, and his wealth not plundered until he has been called back. Then, if he refuses, he'll be slain, and his wealth taken as plunder."

60 Or, "He permitted shedding the blood and taking wealth of the disbeliever unless he pays the *jizyah* tribute or is granted safety for a period." It is clear from the context of this record of a jurisprudential debate on the correct ruling on the wealth of apostates that this Daesh quotation of a clause from a sentence near the end does not accurately represent Imam al-Shafi'i's detailed discussion on when and where it is lawful to attack non-Muslims. The fact that the Daesh propagandists took it from here implies that the more directly relevant section of *Kitab al-Umm* did not serve their purposes.

Soundbite 10: "& the *kafir*'s blood is not spared until he becomes a Muslim."

IMAM SHAAFI (R) SAID, "& THE KAFIR'S BLOOD IS NOT SPARED UNTIL HE BECOMES A MUSLIM."-AL UMM[61]

C10/1 al-Shafi'i[62] – may Allah the Exalted have mercy upon him – said, "If rebels appear in any Muslim country, and their leader executes any of prescribed penalties, be it for Allah's sake or for that of the people, and he was correct in executing it; or if the rebel leader takes in full whatever zakat is due from the Muslims, or he takes what is due from them and more besides, and after that the people of just cause vanquish them, they should not return to whomever the rebel leader executed a prescribed penalty on, nor to whomever they took the zakat from by charging a general zakat. However, if zakat was due from the population, and the rebels took part of it, then the leader of the people of just cause may take whatever remains of it after subtracting whatever the rebels took of it." He added, "Likewise whoever passes by the rebels, and they take that as a tax from him."

C10/2 He said, "If the leader of the people of just cause wishes to take zakat from the people of rebellion, and they claim that the leader of the people of rebellion has already taken it from them, then they are deemed responsible for their zakat. However, if the just leader suspects any of them of lying, he should ask him to swear on oath. If he swears on oath, he must not to be charged zakat again. Likewise for whatever the rebels

61 See https://shamela.ws/book/1655/1089 (viewed 20/05/2025) for the Arabic text of *Qala al-Shafi'i rahimahu Allah ta'ala wa-idha zahara ahl al-baghy 'ala balad min buldan al-Muslimin*.

62 In the printed edition, this section is headed *Ruling on the property, etc., of those who rebel*, showing that, once again, the Daesh propagandists chose to take out of context a remark from a section that does not deal with the shedding of hostile non-Muslims' blood, but with the property of Muslim rebels, or rebels from any protected non-Muslim communities in Muslim lands. The intended reader of al-Shafi'i's *Kitab al-Umm*, would have known to look elsewhere in the book for a detailed description of the rules pertaining the treatment of hostile non-Muslims. However, the presumption appears to be that the target reader of Daesh propaganda will be satisfied with just the author's name, the title of the book, and the easily digested 'soundbite', because he or she lacks either the education or the inclination to refer to the original text – or even a translation of it – and to question and test whether the intended inference of the decontextualised soundbite is correct.

took by way of land tax or *jizyah* poll tax, he must not be charged again for whatever the rebels took from him because they are Muslims whose ruling is upheld in whatever location they took it. No further charge is required of them, be it in land tax or the *jizyah* poll tax or any other fee due for payment in wealth or anything else."

C10/3 He said, "If the leader of the people of rebellion appoints a man to be a cadi, then he must act in accordance with what is required of a cadi in terms of enforcing the right of certain people over others, be it in prescribed penalty or other cases, if he is entrusted with that. If the people of just cause vanquish the people of rebellion, nothing of the ruling of the judge of the people of rebellion should be overturned except what would cause the ruling of other judges to be overturned, namely going against the Book of God, the Sunnah, popular consensus or whatever equates to that, or a deliberate prejudice in rejecting the testimony of the people of just cause at the time when he rejected it, or permitting unjust testimony at the time when he permitted it. If a judge of the people of rebellion writes to a judge of the people of just cause regarding a right established in his presence of one man against another who is not of the people of rebellion then, generally in this case, there is a fear that he will reject the testimony of the people of just cause that goes against his opinion and will accept the testimony of one who is unjust by agreeing with him; and among them are those who it is feared declare lawful on some occasions seizing the property of people where possible. My preference is that he does not accept his written injunction, as his written injunction is not a ruling issued by him. So, the just cadi has no right to reject it except if some perversion of justice is evident to him. However, if the rebel cadi and witnesses can be trusted as regards what I have described,[63] free from every trace of it, and if the cadi wrote from a distant land, such that the right of the beneficiary of the testimony would be extinguished if he were to reject the written injunction, and the cadi accepts his rebel peer's written injunction, then there is a basis for that; but Allah knows best. The written injunction of the rebels' cadi is equivalent to what his own

63 i.e. from seeking to pervert the course of justice.

ruling would be on the matter, if it is as I have described, in that rejecting it would result in rights being neglected."

C10/4 He said, "Whoever from the people of rebellion testifies before a judge of the people of just cause whilst his status is that of a belligerent, or he is from amongst those who considers their opinion as other than belligerence, if he is known for declaring lawful some of what I have described, including testifying in favour of someone who agrees with him: [1] by confirming what he has neither seen nor heard; [2] by declaring lawful the seizing of the property of the person being testified against or the shedding of his blood; [3] whatever factor other than that by which he seeks a means to benefit the one in favour of whom he is testifying; or [4] to harm the one against whom he is testifying, then his testimony is inadmissible regarding anything, no matter how negligible. However, whoever from amongst the people of rebellion or others is innocent of this and is fair, his testimony is admissible."

C10/5 He said, "If it occurs that a man of the rebel camp has a right over a man from the camp of the people of just cause, be it in retribution for a life or an injury, or in relation to property, a cadi of the people of just cause must enforce that right on his behalf. There is no difference between either in what right may be enforced on behalf of some from others in terms of inheritance or whatever else. Likewise, the cadi of the people of rebellion is required to enforce the right of a Muslim or any other non-rebel on his behalf against a rebel. If the cadi of the people of rebellion were to refuse to enforce a legal right against one of them on behalf of someone who opposes them, we would deem him on that basis to be a wrongdoer. Nor is it proper for a cadi of the people of just cause to prevent members of the people of rebellion from asserting their legal rights against members of the people of just cause simply because the rebel cadi withheld their right from them."

C10/6 He said, "Likewise, that rebel-appointed cadi may enforce a right against the people of just cause on behalf of the people of war and of protected non-Muslims. If the people of war withhold a right, then they will be guilty of wrongdoing. The people most worthy of showing patience in achieving their rights from the people of the religion of Allah the Exalted are the people of the Sunnah. Nor does the withholding by the leader of the associators of a Muslim's right over someone within that leader's grasp make it lawful for the Muslim to withhold a right from an enemy associator who has been granted safety, because he is not the one who wronged the Muslim and so deserves to be detained tit for tat. One does not withhold a right from a man by wronging someone else." And al-Shafi'i adopted this opinion.[64]

C10/7 He said, "If the people of rebellion take a city, and they appoint to the judiciary a man of a community known for its opposition to the political opinion of the people of rebellion, and he writes to another cadi, the case should be looked into. If the former cadi is just, and if he names witnesses whom the cadi addressed in his letter knows personally, or whom, prior to receipt of the letter, people of equity already knew to be fair and opposed to the people of rebellion, even if they do not know him but his letter is, as I have described, from those of a cadi of the people of rebellion."

C10/8 He said, "If the people of rebellion attack the associators simultaneously with the people of just cause, and they meet in the associators' lands, join forces and fight alongside each other, and if each of the two groups has a leader, then the people of rebellion and those of justice, their respective armies and each individual amongst them are alike in everything relating to booty but not the fifth due to the caliph."

C10/9 He said, "If one of them grants safety to any of the rebels, be it a slave, a freeman or a woman, then that guarantee of safety is enforceable. If one of them should kill during the advance, he has a share of the spoils. If the people of rebellion are in a camp supporting the people of just cause, and the people of just cause attack their shared non-Muslim enemy by night and seize booty, or if the people of just cause are in a camp

64 The opinion described here as held by al-Shafi'i, effectively that "Two wrongs don't make a right," appears to be the exact opposite of the argument used by extremists to attempt to justify perpetrating atrocities. As the Qur'an states in verses in five different suras, (Q.6:164 et al.) *{... no burden bearer will bear another sinner's burden}*.

supporting the people of rebellion, and the people of rebellion attack their non-Muslim enemy by night and seize booty, each of the two parties should let the other share in it. They should not act separately except that the leader of the people of just cause is more deserving of the fifth share of the booty because it is for him to distribute to people scattered across the Muslim lands, since his rule has sway over them, unlike that of the rebel leader. Thus, it should not be deemed lawful to retain it because the rebel leader considers it so."

C10/10 He said, "If the people of rebellion enter into a truce with a people from among the associators, no one from among the Muslims has the right to attack those associators. If he were to attack them and so take something from them, he must return it to them.[65] Likewise, if the people of rebellion attack a people that the leader of the Muslims has entered into a truce with, and the people of rebellion take them captive, if the Muslims gain victory over the people of rebellion, they should remove that which was seized from their clutches and return it to its associator owners." He said, "Purchasing any of those captives is unlawful. If a Muslim does so, his purchase is void."[66]

C10/11 He said, "If the people of rebellion seek the support of the people of war to fight the people of just cause, and if the people of just cause had previously entered into a truce with the people of war, then it is lawful for the people of just cause to fight the people of war and to take them captive. In that case, the fact of their being in league with the Muslim people of rebellion is not an absolute guarantee of security, rather that they have a guarantee of security in return for abstaining from attacking. However, by fighting the people of just cause, even though they had a guarantee of security but nevertheless fight the people of just cause, then that constitutes a breach of it. It may also be

---

65 In other words, even if a Muslim is convinced of the validity of the so-called Islamic state and its claim that its leader is the rightful caliph, it is unlawful for him to attack those non-Muslims with whom the 'rebel' leaders, who happen to rule over the majority of the world's Muslims, have entered into peace treaties.

66 This point relates directly to the atrocities that occur in non-Muslim lands that have peace treaties with the rulers of Muslim lands, where civilians are maimed and killed.

said, 'If the people of rebellion seek the support of protected non-Muslims to fight the Muslims, that does not count as a breach of covenant because they are still with a group of Muslims.' I am of the opinion that if they were coerced or claim ignorance, saying, 'We thought that we were required, if one group of Muslims conscripted us to fight against another group of Muslims, they are only conscripting us to fight against those whose blood it is lawful to shed in Islam,' such as highwaymen; or saying, 'We did not know that those whom they conscripted us to fight against were Muslims,' that does not constitute a breach of their covenant. However, they will be held of account for all that they took from the people of just cause in terms of the shedding of blood and seizing of property. That is because they are not of the believers that Allah commanded us to reconcile between them."[67] al-Shafi'i – may Allah the Exalted have mercy upon him – added, "We should approach them and renew their covenant with a condition on them that if they enter into the like of this again, it will be lawful to kill them. And I ask Allah for success."

C10/12 He said, "If anyone from the people of rebellion comes over to the side of the people of just cause and is repentant, retribution short not be exacted from him because he is a Muslim whose blood is inviolable. If protected non-Muslims fight alongside the people of just cause against the people of war, they are not given any of the booty, nor of the fifth distributed by the leader of the Muslims, nor a share. Instead they should get a small gift."

C10/13 He said, "If the people of rebellion send to the people of just cause a group from among themselves as hostages, and the people of just cause do likewise, and they say to each other, 'Detain our hostages until we send you back your hostages,' and they enter into a truce over that for a period agreed between them, but then the people of rebellion transgress against the hostages from the people of just cause and kill them, the people of just cause do not have the right to kill the hostages that they hold from the people of rebellion, nor may they

67 See Q.49:9-10.

continue to detain them once they have established that their companions have been killed, since their companions will never be sent back to them. Hostages should not be killed for the crime of others. If the hostages from the people of rebellion remain with equivalent hostages from the people of just cause, and they had entered into a truce for a given period, and that period comes to an end with the people of rebellion having acted treacherously, the people of just cause do not have the right to detain the hostages further due to the treachery of others.

C10/14 He said, "If the people of just cause guarantee the safety of a man from the people of rebellion, and an ignorant man kills him, then his blood money is payable. However, if the person of just cause kills the rebel with intent, and the killer is the heir of the victim or vice versa, I am not of the opinion that either should inherit from the other; but Allah knows best. Their heirs, excluding the killers themselves, should inherit from both of them jointly. If members of the people of rebellion are killed in battle or in other circumstances, the funeral prayer should be performed over them. That is because the prayer is a sunnah amongst the Muslims except for the martyr whom the associators kill in battle, whose body should neither be washed nor prayed over. As for the people of rebellion, if they are killed in battle, they should be washed, prayed over, and treated as the Muslim dead should generally be treated. Their heads should not be sent to some other place; neither should their bodies be crucified, nor should they be denied burial. In contrast, if the people of rebellion kill the people of just cause in battle then, regarding them, there are two opinions. First, they should be buried with their wounds, blood, and the clothes that they were killed in, if they wish, because they are martyrs; nor should they be prayed over but rather treated like those killed by the associators, because they were killed in battle and hence are martyrs. Second, that they should be prayed over. This is because the basis of the ruling amongst Muslims is that the funeral prayer is due over the dead except where Allah's Messenger PBUH abstained from performing it, and he only abstained from it regarding those whom the associators killed in battle."

C10/15 al-Shafi'i – may Allah the Exalted have mercy upon him – said, "The women and children of the people of rebellion, if they are killed with them, then, regarding the prayer over them, it is like over adult males."

C10/16 He said, "I detest that a man of the people of just cause should deliberately kill one of his kinsfolk from amongst the people of rebellion. Moreover, if he should hold back from killing his father, one of his kinsfolk or his brother from amongst the associators, I do not detest him doing that; rather I love him for it. That is because the Prophet PBUH held Abu Hudhayfah ibn 'Utbah back from killing his father and also Abu Bakr, on the day of Uhud, from killing his father.[68] If the dissident group were to kill some of the people of the *qiblah* who declared themselves separate other than on the basis of a strange interpretation of scripture, or they seize property, then the ruling regarding them is the ruling applied to highwaymen; and that is written down in the *Book of brigandry*. If a group of people were to revert from Islam to disbelief, and they were then to join together and fight such that they killed and seized property, then the ruling regarding them is the ruling applied to the people of war amongst the associators. If they were to repent, they should not be pursued over any blood shed or property seized. If someone asks, 'Why shouldn't they be pursued?' they should be told, 'These people became hostile combatants whose property and blood it is lawful to seize or shed. There is no retribution over whatever such combatants take, nor is whatever is taken from them returned to them. For example, Tulayhah killed 'Ukashah ibn Muhsin and Thabit ibn Aqram, and after that he accepted Islam, and he was not subjected either to payment of blood money or to retribution."

C10/17 al-Shafi'i – may Allah the Exalted have mercy upon him – said, "The prescribed penalties are to be applied equally for unlawful use of force

68 The Battle of Uhud occurred in 3/625, three years before the Treaty of Hudaybiyah in 6/628, which is when 'Umar ibn al-Khattab urged Abu Jandal to kill his father, telling him, "Be patient, Abu Jandal, for they are merely *mushrikeen* and their blood is nothing but like the blood of a dog." Later, however, the narrators of the hadith reported that 'Umar used to say, "I have not ceased to fast, give in charity, to pray, and to free slaves due to what I did, out of fear of the words that I uttered that day, hoping that it would be good for me in the hereafter." (See para. C18/7 below.)

in urban and desert areas. Indeed, it may be that those who use violence in cities are worse sinners." al-Rabi' added, "Another statement of al-Shafi'i's is that one should retaliate against them if they turn apostate and use violence and kill people, since associating other gods with God, even if it does not make them worse, neither does withholding from retaliating against them make them any better."

C10/18 al-Shafi'i – may Allah the Exalted have mercy upon him – said, "If the party of rebellion take over a city, and another group of rebels wish to fight them, I am not of the opinion that the people of the city should fight with them. If they say, 'We will fight you together,' then it is permitted for the people of the city to fight them in self-defence and to defend their dependents and property. In that case, if Allah wills, they may be considered amongst those killed protecting their lives and wealth. If the associators take the rebellious Muslim party captive, and if the Muslims have the power to fight the associators, then the Muslims are not permitted to hold back from fighting the associators in order to rescue the rebels.[69] If the Muslims attack the associators, and their governor dies, and they attack together with the rebels or separately, and each of them then returns to their leader, each of them should give their leader a share of the booty."

C10/19 al-Shafi'i – may Allah the Exalted have mercy upon him – said, "Someone asked me, 'What do you say of the person intent on seizing a man's property, shedding his blood, or violating his wife?' I told him, 'That man is permitted to repel him from them.' He asked, 'What if he can only repel them by fighting?' I replied, 'Then he should fight him.' He said, 'Even if the fighting imperils his own life?' 'Yes,' I said, 'if that is the only way to repel his assailant.' He asked, 'And what is the meaning of being able to repel him by other means than that?' I replied, 'If he is on horseback, and his assailant is on foot, intent on taking the horse; or he is in a fortified place and closes the fort for a while till the danger passes. However, if his assailant insists on laying siege to him and fighting him,

69 In other words, any requirement to attack enemy territory is conditional on both the necessary strength AND the presence of Muslim prisoners of war, even if they were rebels.

then he too should fight.' He said, 'Did not Hammad mention from Yahya ibn Sa'id, from Abu Umamah ibn Sahl ibn Hunayf, that 'Uthman ibn 'Affan said that Allah's Messenger PBUH said, "Shedding the blood of a Muslim person is not lawful except in one of three cases: disbelief after faith, fornication after marriage, or taking a life other than in retribution for a life"?' I told him, 'The hadith of 'Uthman as he narrated it and the statement of Allah's Messenger PBUH, "Shedding the blood of a Muslim is not lawful except in one of three cases," as he said it, this is Arabic speech. Its meaning is that if any one of the three occurs, his blood is lawful to be shed, as he said it. Suppose a man had fornicated, then abandoned fornication, repented of it or fled from the location where he had fornicated, and it was possible to arrest him, he should be stoned to death. If he had intentionally killed a Muslim, then abandoned killing, repented and fled, he should be killed in retribution. However, if he had disbelieved and then repented, the label of disbelief would vanish from him, whereas the label of adultery and murder would not leave these other two, even if they repented and fled, they would deserve to be killed due to the label applied to them both. Likewise the disbeliever after having believed, if he were to flee without abandoning the statement of disbelief after having manifested it, he should be killed unless if he repents of his disbelief and returns to Islam, then his blood should be spared. That is because the label of disbelief lapses in his case, if he returns to Islam. So, he is not to be killed if he returns as a Muslim; but, when the label of disbelief applies to him, then he is like the adulterer and the murderer.'"

C10/20 al-Shafi'i – may Allah the Exalted have mercy upon him – said, "Regarding the rebel, it is excessive to say of him that shedding his blood is absolutely permissible without exception. Rather, it may only be said if he rebels and puts up resistance or fights with the people of resistance against the established authority, he may be fought to prevent him killing or to urge him to return or to repay some right that he may have withheld. If he comes back without personally having participated in fighting, then there is no blood money or retribution in respect of him. Whilst we do permit fighting him, if he retreats from the fight, disengages, is injured, is taken captive, or is unable to fight due to sickness, he should not be killed in any of these circumstances. Nor should it be said of a rebel in such a legal position that shedding his blood is lawful. If shedding his blood were lawful in all circumstances, it would not be spared due to his retreating, being taken captive, injuries, or disengaging. Whilst *the kafir's blood is not spared until he becomes a Muslim,*[70] the rebel's legal status, by contrast, is as I have described above regarding the status of a Muslim intent on shedding the blood of another man or seizing his property."

70 This indicates that different rules of engagement exist in the Sharia when confronting combatants who are disbelievers compared to those who are Muslims rebelling against the established authorities. Unlike those vulnerable and untrained Muslims targeted by Daesh propagandists on social media, the intended readers of al-Shafi'i's eight-volume work can reasonably be assumed to have already studied the preceding chapter on the *jizyah* tribute and on fighting disbelievers (*Kitab al-jizyah*), and hence to be familiar with the rules of war relating hostile non-Muslims as opposed to Muslims – and protected non-Muslims – who intend to cause grievous bodily harm or to steal or rob. By way of comparison, the chapter containing the rules of jihad is three times longer than that on fighting Muslim rebels.

Soundbite 11: "The *kafir*, whether he fights the Muslim or not, …"

SHAWKANI (R) SAID, "THE KAFIR, WHETHER HE FIGHTS THE MUSLIM OR NOT, HIS BLOOD IS HALAL TO SPILL AS LONG AS HE IS A KAFIR."-ASSAYLALJARRAR[71]

C11/1 On his statement "Section: And the land of Islam,"[72] etc., I say that account should be taken of the clear presence of the statement of Islamic faith and if the land's commands and prohibitions belong in the hands of the people of Islam such that any disbelievers in it are unable to manifest their disbelief except to the extent that the people of Islam permit them to do so, then that is a land of Islam. Nor does the appearance of some traits of disbelief there detract from that because they do not appear due to the strength of the disbelievers, nor to their offensive capacity, as is observed in the case of the protected peoples, including Jews, Christians and others with treaties, resident in Muslim cities. However, if the situation is the opposite, then the land too is the opposite.

C11/2 As for his saying, "even by interpretation," as a statement, it is void, and in terms of opinion, it is nonsensical. Such matters over which the people of Islam have differed with some, out of fanaticism and bigotry born of whim, declaring others to be disbelievers, if their appearance in a land required it to be a land of disbelief, then all Islamic lands would be lands of disbelief on account of their populations.[73] This is because there is not a single Islamic town or city that is devoid of adherents of the Ash'ari, Mu'tazilite or Maturidi doctrines; and each of these groups holds beliefs

71 See https://shamela.ws/book/7342/1062 for the Arabic text of *Fasl wa-dar al-Islam ma zaharat fihi al-shahadatan wa-al-salah*. (For information about this commentary, see footnotes on C6 above.)

72 The section of the Zaydi text *al-Azhar* commented on here by al-Shawkani reads in full: "Section: And the land of Islam is wherever the two statements of faith and the ritual prayer are apparent, and where no trait of disbelief is apparent, even by interpretation, except due to proximity to the land of disbelief. If not, then it is a land of disbelief even if, on the contrary, those two traits of Islam are apparent; and it is necessary to emigrate from it and from the land of blatant wrongdoing to a place devoid – or at least with less – of whatever he and his family are emigrating from, except if there be some benefit or excuse, and it is restricted by the command of the Muslim ruler."

73 Here al-Shawkani presents a terse but logical argument against the *takfiri* tendencies of extremists whose declarations effectively make apostates of the overwhelming majority who either disagree with them or accept the authority of scholars who disagree with them.

that the other group deems disbelief by interpretation. It is bad enough for you to hear such utterances. The truth is that there is no such thing as disbelief by interpretation in any case, but this is not the place to expand on this issue. So, take it in its entirety and save yourself thereby from innumerable sins and unlimited perils. Below, in the discussion of his statement "& the interpreter is like an apostate",[74] will appear whatever is proper to be added to what appears here in order to complete the lesson.

C11/3 Know that juxtaposing mention of the land of Islam with the land of disbelief is of very little use for the reason we presented to you earlier in the discussion of the land of war, and that **it is permissible** to shed **the blood of the enemy disbeliever and** to seize his **wealth in all circumstances, so long as he has not obtained a guarantee of safety**[75] **from the Muslims**, whereas the blood and wealth of the Muslim are inviolable due to the inviolability granted on the basis of Islam be it in the land of war or elsewhere. If the lesson to be drawn from this is what was mentioned earlier that they have control over us to the extent of whatever enters their land by force then, as we made clear to you there, they have no control over us. However, if the lesson is the requirement to emigrate from the land of disbelief, then this requirement is not peculiar to the land of disbelief but rather is a standing order (*sharia*) and an established custom (*sunnah*) whenever wrongdoing comes to light, and it is impossible to uphold the requirement to enjoin good and forbid evil, or when no one exists who is ready and able to seize hold of the hands of those who violate Allah's prohibitions. It is therefore right that Allah's believing servant should save himself by fleeing with his

74 Al-Shawkani's detailed discussion of this phrase appears a few pages later towards the very end of the book, where he writes, "On this I say that here words pour forth as he bemoans the state of Islam and its people that his religious fanaticism has provoked him to inflict on the overwhelming majority of Muslims due to the build-up of disbelief not in relation either to the Sunnah or the Qur'an, nor any explanation from Allah or proof, but simply due to the boiling over of the cauldrons of his sectarian bigotry..."

75 It seems that whoever translated this sentence as "The kafir, whether he fights the Muslim or not, his blood is halal to spill as long as he is a kafir" for propaganda purposes misread *lam yu'man* (i.e. he has not been granted safety, or he has no guarantee of safe passage) as *lam yu'min* (i.e. he does not believe, hence "he is a kafir").

religion intact, if he is able, to find a land free of the manifestation of acts of disobedience against Allah, whose perpetrators go unchecked. If he finds no such place, then the best possible course is to remain, enjoining what is right and forbidding wrong by his hand or, if he cannot, with his tongue or, if he cannot even do that, in his heart, as the truthful, believed Prophet PBUH indicated in an authenticated statement of his. Thereafter, if he is able to shut the door on himself to place a barrier between himself and the disobedient wrongdoers, then that is the least of what is required of him. I have clarified the issue of emigration, whatever aspect of it remains in force and what has been abrogated, in my commentary on *al-Muntaqa*,[76] which should be referred to.[77]

C11/4 As for what the author mentioned by way of imitation, asserting a land of flagrant wrongdoing exists as a new category for whoever among the Mu'tazilites deviates from orthodoxy, there is no basis at all for that, nor is that any benefit in it, even if one who lacks insight claims it to be so.

C11/5 As for his saying, "to a place devoid of whatever he and his family are emigrating from," it is self-evident since moving from one evil to another, or from one land of disobedient sinners to another such land entails nothing but exhausting oneself by crossing deserts. However, if the appearance of sinful disobedience elsewhere is less than it is in his homeland, that is a valid reason for emigrating, as there is a choice between greater and lesser evil.

C11/6 As for his saying, "except if there be some benefit," its explanation too is self-evident. So, if the benefit accrues to one group of Muslims by its remaining is self-evident, such as when he has some means to enjoin good and forbid wrong,[78] or to teach the principles of goodness so that

---

76 Here al-Shawkani is referring to his commentary *Nayl al-awtar sharh Muntaqá al-akhbar*, on a collection of authentic hadiths containing legal rulings, compiled by Ibn Taymiyah's grandfather, 'Abd al-Salam ibn 'Abd Allah (d.652-1254).

77 On this basis, a reasonable person reading the whole text might deem it prudent to study this additional work before deciding to act on the decontextualised – and mistranslated – soundbite picked for propaganda purposes by Daesh.

78 It is interesting to consider whether al-Shawkani would have included in this those Muslims in non-Muslim-majority lands today who engage in local or national politics, or in the administration of justice, with the intention of improving society and reducing crime.

that is preferable to emigrating and fleeing with his religion intact, then he should abandon emigration in order to take care of this preferable benefit. That is because this achievable benefit for him personally becomes a negative factor compared to the anticipated benefit of his abandoning emigration to help the community.

C11/7 As for emigration being restricted by the command of the Muslim ruler regarding it, its explanation is found in what we wrote above on the requirement to obey rulers in what they command; and there is ample evidence of that in the Qur'an and Sunnah.

Soundbite 12: "It is the existence of *kufr* that permits the blood."

IBN HAJAR (R) SAID, "IT IS THE EXISTENCE OF KUFR THAT PERMITS THE BLOOD."-FATHULBAARI[79]

C12/1 His saying, "Chapter: A Muslim is not to be killed for a disbeliever."[80] He chose for this subsection to follow the one before it[81] to indicate that [a] the severe injunction against killing a dhimmi does not extend to retribution against a Muslim who kills him intentionally; and [b] a Muslim, even if he is not killed in retribution for a disbeliever, does not have the right to kill every disbeliever but rather that he is forbidden from killing without a valid claim the dhimmi and the one covered by a treaty.

C12/2 His saying "Sadaqah ibn al-Fadl told us" is established in some copies. Here it appears as "Ahmad ibn Yunus told us, Zuhayr told us, Mutarrif told us that 'Amir told them from Abu Juhayfah..." and elsewhere it appears "Sadaqah ibn al-Fadl told us," etc.; and the correct form is what is in most copies. The narration via Ahmad ibn Yunus has already appeared in the Book of the *Jizyah* Tribute. His saying "Mutarrif" appears without diacritics, but the letter *ra'* is doubled, and he is the highly esteemed son of Tarif, the famous Kufi scholar.

---

79 See https://shamela.ws/book/1673/7248 (viewed 26/05/2025) for the Arabic text of Ibn Hajar al-'Asqalani's commentary on hadith no. 6915 in *Sahih al-Bukhari*, the translation of which reads: Ahmad ibn Yunus told us, Zuhayr told us, Mutarrif told us that 'Amir told them from Abu Juhayfah, who said, 'I said to 'Ali.' Sadaqah ibn al-Fadl told us, Ibn 'Uyaynah told us, Mutarrif told us, I heard al-Sha'bi tell, 'I heard Abu Juhayfah say, "I asked 'Ali – may Allah be pleased with him – 'Have you anything additional in writing that isn't in the Qur'an?'" and on one occasion Ibn 'Uyaynah said, "that is not with the people?" 'Ali replied, 'By Him Who causes the seed to split and gave life to each creature that breathes, apart from what is in the Qur'an, nothing except the faculty of understanding that a man may be given of His Book and what is on this sheet.' I asked, 'And what is on that sheet?' He replied, 'Rules relating to blood money, ransom for captives, and that a Muslim is not to be killed in retribution for a disbeliever.'"

80 This quotation is from a chapter on retribution in *Fath al-Bari sharh Sahih al-Bukhari*, not from the chapter on jihad as war or on the conduct of war. This is clear from the text of the hadith with its reference to the limits established in the Sharia to retribution against a Muslim who has killed a disbeliever.

81 i.e. the chapter on the sin of whoever kills a blameless dhimmi (*Bab ithm man qatala dhimmi bi-ghayr jurm*). As this first paragraph makes clear, this hadith certainly does not consist of a general ruling permitting a Muslim to shed any disbeliever's blood, as implied by the propagandists' decontextualised soundbite.

C12/3 Regarding his saying "I asked 'Ali", the explanation of the reason for this question has already appeared in the chapter *The Book of Knowledge*. This version is shorter than the version of it in *The Book of Knowledge* from another form, narrated from Mutarrif that Ahmad said from Sufyan ibn 'Uyaynah, with this chain of transmission, "'Do you have anything from Allah's Messenger PBUH?' He did not hesitate but said, 'No, by Him Who causes the seed to split and gave life to each creature that breathes, nothing except the faculty of understanding of the Qur'an that Allah gives a man and what is on this sheet,'" which he then mentioned. This appeared earlier from another form from Mutarrif in the Book of Knowledge and elsewhere with a commentary on the hadith and an explanation of the differences in wording that I have transcribed from 'Ali, and an explanation of the intended meaning of rules relating to blood money, ransom for captives.

C12/4 As for desisting from killing a Muslim in retribution for a disbeliever, the majority of scholars have taken to ruling on that basis except that, based on the statement of Malik on brigands and whoever fits the label, if he kills in cold blood, he should be killed even if the victim is a protected non-Muslim as an exception to this general rule of preventing the killing of a Muslim for a disbeliever. This is because there is another key point, namely that of wreaking havoc in the land.[82] The Hanafi school took an opposite stance, saying that a Muslim is to be killed in retribution for a protected non-Muslim if he kills him unlawfully, but he is not to be killed in retribution for an enemy disbeliever granted safe passage. From al-Sha'bi and al-Nakh'i, it is reported that a Muslim is to be killed in retribution for a Jew or a Christian, but not a Zoroastrian; and they quoted in evidence what occurs in Abu Dawud's writings via al-Hasan, from Qays ibn 'Ubad, from 'Ali, with the wording "A believer is not killed in retribution for disbeliever, nor is anyone with a valid covenant." Abu Dawud also recorded it from 'Amr ibn Shu'ayb's narration, from his

82 From this perspective, one can argue that, like brigandry or highway robbery, terrorist atrocities that target civilians in public places fit the label *{wreaking havoc in the land}* in the Qur'an (Q.5:32) regardless of any ideological spin put on them by the perpetrators. Therefore, technically, it does not breach the broad scholarly convention disapproving of the killing of a Muslim in retribution for a non-Muslim, since the crime ceases to be simple murder.

father, from his grandfather. Ibn Majah recorded it from a hadith narrated by Ibn 'Abbas; likewise, al-Bayhaqi from 'A'ishah and Mu'qil ibn Yasar. All these ways of transmitting are weak except the first and second, whose chains of transmission are sound and worthy of acceptance.

C12/5 The scholars have said that the reason for quoting this in evidence is that it is deemed to mean "and anyone with a valid covenant is not to be killed in retribution for a disbeliever." They also said it has to do with the connecting of the specific to the general; and it needs to be specified because the only disbeliever in retribution for whom anyone with a valid covenant would otherwise be killed is the enemy disbeliever, who is not his equal or higher in status; and the only one who is killed in retribution for the non-Muslim with a covenant is the enemy disbeliever. So, due to the semantic equivalence of the two connected terms, the disbeliever in retribution for whom a Muslim is not to be killed is only the hostile one.

C12/6 Al-Tahawi[83] said, "If the sense of the hadith had been to deny the killing of a Muslim in retribution for a protected non-Muslim, then the form of wording would have been to say, "nor in retribution for anyone with a valid covenant," otherwise it would have been a grammatical error, and the Prophet PBUH did not make grammatical errors. Given that the wording is as it is and not like that suggested, we know that anyone with a valid covenant is meant in retribution; so, the inference is that neither the believer nor anyone with a valid covenant is to be killed in retribution for a disbeliever." Al-Tahawi added, "And a similar example is found in the Qur'an (Q.65:4) *{& those of your womenfolk who have reached the menopause, if you are in doubt, then their waiting period is three months; and those who have not yet menstruated}* where the inference is that the waiting period is equal for those who no longer menstruate and those who have yet to menstruate." Al-Tahawi then reassessed that the root meaning is the absence of inference, and that the wording stands without it, if we take the later clause as resuming

83 Abu Ja'far al-Tahawi (d.321/933) was an Egyptian Hanafi and hadith scholar. This paragraph appears to be a paraphrase from al-Tahawi's *Sharh ma'ani al-athar*.

the sense of the initial clause.[84] Supporting this explanation is the fact that the authentic hadith confines itself to the first sentence. Even if one accepts that the syntax's purpose is to connect two clauses, any association is in relation to the negation element, not in every aspect. It is like when someone says, "I passed by Zayd as he was setting off and 'Amr." It is not necessary that 'Amr too was setting off, rather that the association between Zayd and 'Amr is in the element of my passing by them.

C12/7 Al-Tahawi also said that it is incorrect to impose this meaning on the resuming clause because the context of the hadith as regards shedding the blood of different categories of people, some of which cause the other to be void since, in some of its ways of narration, the blood of Muslims is on a par with that of non-Muslims. He then reassessed the matter, concluding that this limitation of the meaning should be resisted, as there are a great many rulings other than this in the hadith. Al-Shafi'i revealed its particular relevance, saying that it is as though when the Prophet PBUH let his companions know that there was to be no retribution between them and the disbelievers, he also let them know that they were forbidden to shed unlawfully the blood of protected non-Muslims and of people with whom Muslims had a covenant. So, he PBUH said a Muslim is not to be killed for a disbeliever, nor should a non-Muslim person with a valid covenant be killed, and the meaning of the hadith is that Muslim is not to be killed in retribution for a disbeliever, nor should whoever has a covenant be killed in retribution for a disbeliever so long as his covenant remains valid. Ibn al-Sam'ani said that, as for their applying the hadith to an enemy disbeliever granted safe passage, it is incorrect because the lesson it contains should accord with the generality of the utterance until evidence to be more specific presents itself. As regards the meaning,

---

84 In other words, in this Qur'anic example (Q.65:4), there is an initial clause (paraphrased as "the waiting period of those of your womenfolk who have reached the menopause is three months"), and a clause in which the waiting period theme is resumed (again paraphrased as "the waiting period of those who have not yet menstruated is also three months"). Similarly with the original hadith ("A believer is not killed in retribution for disbeliever, nor is anyone with a valid covenant to be killed in retribution for a disbeliever.")

the general rule which is constructed in law on Islam and disbelief is either due to the honour of Islam or the deficiency of disbelief, or both together. Islam is the source of honour and disbelief of ignominy. Furthermore, to permit shedding the blood of a protected non-Muslim on the grounds that it is the existence of *kufr* that permits the blood[85] is obvious sophistry;[86] and that a non-Muslim's protected status is just an obstructive covenant that prevents killing despite the cause for the shedding of blood remaining. One aspect of loyalty to the covenant is that a Muslim must not kill a protected non-Muslim. Although the issue of the killing is agreed upon, the statement does not refer to retribution because the sophistry permitting the killing of any disbeliever exists; and so long as the sophistry stands, the issue of retribution will not be referred to.

C12/8 I, Ibn Hajar, have said, "Abu 'Ubayd mentioned with an authentic chain of transmission from Zufar that he dissociated himself from his colleagues' statement and instead relied on the chain of transmission from 'Abd al-Wahid ibn Ziyad, saying, 'I said to Zufar that you say that prescribed penalties may be averted due to doubts. Then you have come upon the greatest of doubtful arguments, on the basis of which you have gone beyond even them suggesting a believer is to be killed for a disbeliever.' Then he said, 'So, bear witness that I have renounced this teaching.'"

C12/9 Ibn al-'Arabi mentioned that some Hanafi scholars asked al-Shashi[87] for the evidence for abandoning killing a Muslim in retribution for a disbeliever. al-Shashi replied, intending to draw his conclusion in general terms, saying, "I apply it specifically to the enemy disbeliever."

---

85 Or, "the existence of disbelief permits the shedding of blood..."

86 According to the English version of the Arabic dictionary of Hans Wehr, the word *shubhah* means: "obscurity, vagueness, uncertainty; doubt; suspicion (esp. of criminal offense; *jur.*); specious argument, sophism; judicial error (*Isl. law*)." Lane's Arabic lexicon defines the word as "confusedness, dubiousness." The compound *qa'im al-shubhah*, which fits here, means "highly questionable, obviously suspect." Only by omitting this are Daesh propagandists able to present as fact what the scholar whom they quoted clearly deemed questionable.

87 This is perhaps Nizam al-Din Abu Ali Ahmad ibn Muhammad ibn Ishaq al-Shashi (d.344/955), the author of the well-known Hanafi work on jurisprudence, *Usul al-Shashi*.

al-Shashi then digressed from that, saying, "The basis of my evidence is the Sunnah and its explanation, because mention of an attribute in the ruling demands an explanation. So, the meaning of 'A believer is not to be killed for a disbeliever' is to give preference to the Muslim due to his Islam," and thus he silenced him. Amongst on the basis of which the Hanafis argued is what al-Daraqutni recorded by way of 'Ammar ibn Matar, from Ibrahim ibn Abi Yahya, from Rabi'ah, from Ibn al-Baylamani, from 'Umar, who said that Allah's Messenger PBUH had a Muslim killed in retribution for a disbeliever, saying, "I am the most entitled of all who are loyal to their covenant of protection." However, al-Daraqutni himself said, "Ibrahim ibn Abi Yahya is a weak narrator." No one other than him considered the hadith's chain of transmission connected; and the chain of the famous narration from Ibn al-Baylamani is incomplete. Al-Bayhaqi said, "The narrator 'Ammar ibn Matar erred over Ibrahim in the chain of transmission, as Ibrahim only narrated it from Muhammad ibn al-Munkadir, from 'Abd al-Rahman ibn al-Baylamani. That is the origin on this matter, and the chain of transmission is disjointed; plus its narrator is unreliable." That too is how al-Shafi'i and Abu 'Ubayd together recorded it from Ibrahim ibn Muhammad ibn Abi Yahya.

C12/10 I, Ibn Hajar, have said, "Ibrahim was not alone in narrating it, as his words suggest. Abu Dawud recorded it in his collection of hadiths with incomplete chains of transmission, as did al-Tahawi by way of Sulayman ibn Bilal, from Rabi'ah, from Ibn al-Baylamani. As for Ibn al-Baylamani, a great many have declared him weak, though honest. He is not used in evidence where he is the sole narrator, even if the chain of transmission is complete, so what about if it is incomplete, or where he differs from others?" al-Daraqutni also said that; and, after retelling the hadith from Ibrahim, Abu 'Ubayd mentioned, "It has reached me that Ibrahim said, 'I retold it from Rabi'ah, from Ibn al-Munkadir, from Ibn al-Baylamani; and that is how the hadith returned to Ibrahim, but Ibrahim is also a weak transmitter.'" Abu 'Ubayd said, "And on such a chain of transmission as this, the blood of Muslims is not to be spilt." I, Ibn Hajar, have said, "And it has become apparent that 'Ammar ibn Matar stumbled in his chain of transmission." Al-Shafi'i mentioned an account in *Kitab al-Umm*,[88] the purport of which was that, as regards the Ibn al-Baylamani hadith, it was about an enemy disbeliever granted safe passage, whom 'Amr ibn Umayyah had killed. Al-Shafi'i said, "On this basis, even if it is established as sound, then it is abrogated because the Prophet PBUH preached on the day of the Conquest of Mecca, using the hadith 'A Muslim is not to be killed in retribution for a disbeliever,' as mentioned in the narration of 'Amr ibn Shu'ayb, whereas the story of 'Amr ibn Umayyah preceded that by some time."

C12/11 I, Ibn Hajar, have said, "It is from here that the correctness of the preceding interpretation from al-Shafi'i derives, as the sermon of the Prophet PBUH on the day of the Conquest of Mecca was due to the victim whom Khuza'ah killed although he had a covenant. So, the Prophet PBUH preached, 'If I were to have a believer killed for a disbeliever, I would certainly have killed him for killing this man,' and he said, 'Neither is a believer to be killed for a disbeliever, nor one who has a valid covenant.' In the first ruling, he indicated his abstaining from retribution against al-Khuza'i for the man with a covenant whom he had killed. In the second ruling, he indicated that daring to do what the aforementioned killer had done was prohibited. And Allah knows best. Amongst their arguments is the fact that the hand of the Muslim is amputated for stealing the wealth of a protected non-Muslim; and they said that a life is greater in terms of its inviolability. Ibn Battal answered that it was a sound analogy, were it not for the scriptural text. Others responded that amputating the hand is one of Allah's rights and hence if the theft is repeated exactly as before, the prescribed penalty does not lapse, even if pardoned. Homicide is the opposite of that. Retribution also carries a sense of equivalence, and there is no equivalence for the disbeliever and the Muslim. However, we do not make equivalence a condition in relation to amputation."

88 This refers to a section on the blood money due to protected non-Muslims (*Bab diyat ahl al-dhimmah*), where al-Shafi'i also mentioned a number of reports of retribution by order of the four Rightly Guided Caliphs against Muslims for the intentional killing of a protected non-Muslim, and also referred to the verse (Q.4:92) that makes the blood money for the homicide of a non-Muslim protected by covenant equivalent to that for a Muslim.

Soundbite 13: "If a Muslim meets a *kafir* who has no covenant…"

IMAM QURTUBI (R) SAID, IF A MUSLIM MEETS A KAFIR WHO HAS NO COVENANT, IT IS PERMISSIBLE FOR HIM TO KILL HIM." -TAFSIR QURTUBI[89]

C13/1 (Q.4:94) *{O you who believe, if you strike out on patrol in the path of Allah, clarify and, when someone extends to you a greeting of peace, do not say, "You are not a believer," seeking temporal worldly gain. Prizes aplenty exist with Allah. That is how you used to be before, until Allah favoured you with Islam. So clarify. Allah is ever Aware of what you do.}* On this verse, there are eleven points of interest:

C13/2 First, His Exalted saying *{O you who believe, if you strike out on patrol in the path of Allah, clarify}* This relates to the mention of killing and jihad; and striking out means travelling in the land. The Arabs say, "I struck out in the land when I travel for commerce, battle or other reason" linked to 'in'; and you can say, "I struck the earth" without 'in' when you mean to answer the call of human nature, on which there is the saying of the Prophet PBUH, "Two men should not go out to answer the call of nature, talking to each other and exposing their private parts, for Allah detests that."[90] This verse was revealed in relation to a group of Muslims who, on their journey, passed by a man with a camel and a little flock of sheep that he was selling. He greeted the group and said, "There is no god but Allah. Muhammad is the Messenger of Allah," but, one of them attacked and killed him. When that was mentioned to the Prophet PBUH, it affected him deeply, and the verse was revealed. Al-Bukhari reported it from 'Ata', from Ibn 'Abbas, who said, "Ibn 'Abbas said there was a man amongst his little flock. The Muslims caught up with him. He said, '*al-Salam 'alaykum*!' but they killed him and took his sheep. So, Allah the Exalted revealed that to His words *{temporal worldly gain}* meaning that little flock. He said Ibn 'Abbas recited

89 See https://shamela.ws/book/20855/2006 (viewed 27/05/2025) for the Arabic text of *{Ya ayyuha alladhina amanu idha darabtum fi sabil Allah} fihi ihda 'asharah mas'alah*. The proper title of al-Qurtubi's *tafsir* or commentary is *al-Jami' li-ahkam al-Qur'an* (i.e. *The collection of rulings of the Qur'an*). Both Daesh and Al-Qaeda make selective use of this well-known work to give an air of respectability and authenticity to their truth claims.

90 This hadith, found in *Sunan Abi Dawud*, has been classed as weak.

'*al-Salam*!'" It is recorded in other than al-Bukhari, "and Allah's Messenger PBUH took his blood money to his family and returned his sheep."

C13/3 There was disagreement over identifying the killer and the victim in this incident. According to most, and this is what is in Ibn Ishaq's *Siyar*, Abu Dawud's *Musannaf* & Ibn 'Abd al-Barr's *al-Isti'ab*, the killer was Muhallim ibn Jaththamah, and the victim was 'Amir ibn al-Adbat, and that he PBUH cursed Muhallim, who survived only seven days after that. He was then buried, but the earth rejected him; so he was reburied, but again the earth rejected him. Then was buried for a third time, but the earth rejected him. When they saw that the earth would not accept his corpse, they cast him into one of those ravines. He PBUH said, "The earth certainly does accept worse than him." Al-Hasan said, "As for the earth retaining worse than him, this is true, but he was warning the group off repeating such actions." In Sunan Ibn Majah, from 'Imran ibn Husayn, who said, "Allah's Messenger PBUH sent an army of Muslims against the associators, and they fought them so fiercely that the associators showed them their backs and fled. A man of my own flesh and blood attacked a man of the associators with a spear. When he had overpowered him, the man said, 'I bear witness that there is no god but Allah. I am a Muslim.' But he stabbed and killed him; then he came to Allah's Messenger PBUH and said, 'O Messenger of Allah, I am destroyed.' He PBUH said once or twice, 'What have you done?' and he informed him of what he'd done. Allah's Messenger PBUH asked him, 'Why didn't you split open his belly to know what was in his heart?' He responded, 'O Messenger of Allah, if I had split open his belly, would I have known what was in his heart?' 'No!' said the Prophet PBUH, 'Neither did you accept what he said, nor do you know what was in his heart.' Allah's Messenger PBUH then fell silent. It wasn't long before the man died, and we buried him; but the next morning his corpse was on the surface of the earth. 'Perhaps an enemy disinterred him,' we said, burying him again and ordering our slaves to guard him; but the next morning his corpse was back on the surface of the earth. 'Perhaps our slaves dozed off,' we said, burying him again and this time guarding him ourselves; but the next morning his corpse was again back on the surface of the earth. So, we cast him into one of those ravines."

It has been said that the killer was Usamah ibn Zayd and that the victim was Mirdas ibn Nahik al-Ghatafani al-Farazi from Banu Murrah of the people of Fadak; and Ibn al-Qasim was one of those who said that from Malik. It has also been said, "This particular Mirdas had accepted Islam the night before and had informed his family of that. When the Prophet PBUH made the gravity of the matter clear to Usamah, he swore that he had not fought a man who'd said 'There is no god but Allah,' as previously discussed." It has also been said, "The killer was Abu Qatadah," or else "Abu al-Darda'." There is no dispute, however, that the one whom the earth spat out when he died was Muhallim, as we mentioned. It is possible that all these events occurred around the same time, and that the verse was revealed about all of them. It has been narrated that the Prophet PBUH returned the sheep and the camel to the family of the Muslim, and that he himself bore the cost of his blood money for the sake of maintaining harmony; and Allah knows best. Al-Tha'labi mentioned that the commander of that squadron was Ghalib ibn Fadalah al-Laythi. It has also been said it was al-Miqdad, as told by al-Suhayli.

C13/4 Second, His Exalted saying *{clarify}* means 'Ponder!' And *{fa-tabayyanu}* is the reading of the bulk of scholars, and it is the choice of Abu 'Ubayd and Abu Hatim, who both said, "Whoever is commanded to clarify has been commanded to ascertain the facts." People say, 'I was clear about the matter,' and 'The matter was clear in itself,' both transitive and intransitive. Hamzah recited this word as *{fa-tathabbatu}* with the letter *tha'* with three dots and after it *ba'* with one, but *{fa-tabayyanu}* is more certain in this case, because a person can ascertain but not clarify. The word *{if}* has the meaning of a condition, which is why the letter *fa'* appears in His saying *{fa-tabayyanu}*; and it may be to denote a conditional clause, as in: "If poverty afflicts you, then adorn yourself." The best style is not to denote a conditional clause, as the poet said:

"The soul is desirous, if you wish it to be;
"And if it gets only little, it is content."

To clarify – meaning to ascertain – before deciding whether to kill is obligatory, whether settled in one place or travelling. There is no dispute over this. Travel was only specifically mentioned because the event to which the revelation relates occurred whilst travelling.

C13/5 Third, His Exalted word *{and, when someone extends to you a greeting of peace, do not say, "You are not a believer"}* the Arabic words *al-salam*, *al-silm* and *al-salaam* are all one and the same, as al-Bukhari said, and all of them can be recited.[91] Abu 'Ubayd al-Qasim ibn Sallam chose *{al-salaam}*, but the people of theorisation opposed him, saying *{al-salam}* here is more likely because it has the meaning of compliance and submission, as the Glorious and Majestic said (Q.16:28) *{so, they extended an offer of submission}*, as *al-salam* implies submission and compliance. In other words, "Do not say to whoever offers you his hand and submits to you, manifesting what you are calling to, 'You are not a believer.'" It has been said that *al-salaam* means to say *al-salaam 'alaykum*, which refers back to the first explanation, since his salutation with the greeting of Islam heralds his obedience and compliance. It is also possible what is intended thereby is to be able to withdraw and leave. Al-Akhfash said, "It is said that so-and-so is *salaam* if he mixes with no one." As for *al-silm* with a doubled letter *seen* and the short vowel *i* but no vowel on the letter *laam*, it means [re]conciliation.

C13/6 Fourth, it has been narrated from Abu Ja'far that he recited *{"You are not guaranteed safety"}* with an *a* vowel on the second letter *m* of *mu'manan,* from "You guaranteed his safety when you granted him safe passage, so he was guaranteed safety."[92]

C13/7 Fifth, *if a Muslim meets a kafir who has no covenant,*[93] *it is permissible for him to kill him*. However, if he says, "There is no god but Allah," killing him is not permitted because he has become inviolable through the

91 This refers to the Qur'anic science of *qira'at* or variant 'readings' where traditions survive of the same consonants occasionally being recited with different vowels.

92 This fourth point sheds further light on the Qur'anic science of the different 'readings', where the meaning of the same letters, mostly consonants, can depend on the associated vowels, as here where the usual reading *mu'min* ('believing') contrasts with the rare variant *mu'man* ('granted safety').

93 Any citizen or resident of a non-Muslim country with which any Muslim country has a treaty should be deemed to have a covenant.

inviolability of Islam preventing the shedding of his blood and the seizing of his wealth and family; so if he kills him after that, he should be killed in retribution for him. The ruling to kill those aforementioned in retribution did not apply because they lived at the very start of Islam, and they were of the opinion that the victim only said it to save themselves and out of fear of the weapon, and that protection is only from saying it when calm; but the Prophet PBUH informed them that it guarantees protection however it is said. That is why he asked Usamah, "Didn't you split his heart open to know if he'd said it or not?" as reported by Muslim, meaning to see if he is truthful in saying it or lying. That, of course, is not possible, which leaves only that his tongue should express it. And on this, there is a great category of thought in jurisprudence, namely that rulings are dependent on context and appearances, not on absolute definiteness and uncovering hidden motives.[94]

C13/8 Sixth, if a stranger says, "Peace be upon you," it is also not proper that should be killed until it is known what is behind this because it is problematic. Malik said, "Regarding the disbeliever who, when found, says, 'I have come seeking safety. I request safe passage,' these are difficult matters. I consider that he should be returned to his place of safety, and that he should not be judged as belonging to Islam because his disbelief has been established. It is therefore necessary that what points to the meaning of his words manifests itself from him. It is not sufficient that he say, "I'm a Muslim," or "I'm a believer," or even that he prays, until he utters the protective statement of the faith on which the Prophet PBUH hung the ruling when he said, "I have been commanded to fight the people of this world until they say, 'There is no god but Allah.'"

C13/9 Seventh, if he prays or performs an action peculiar to Islam, our scholars have disputed over it. Ibn al-'Arabi said, "We consider that that does not make him a Muslim unless he is asked, 'What is behind this prayer?' and he answers, 'It is the prayer of a Muslim,' he should be told, 'Say, There is

94 In other words, if a person is clearly heard to pronounce of the first half of the words of the declaration of Islamic faith, the *shahadah*, then he or she must be treated as a Muslim regardless of any suspicions one may harbour about the motive.

no god but Allah.' If he says it, then his truthfulness is clear; but if he refuses, we know that that is trickery. According to whoever considers him a Muslim, this constitutes apostasy; however, the correct opinion is that it is basic disbelief, not apostasy. Likewise, the person who says *Salaam 'alaykum*,[95] should be held responsible to his word. If he said it, his integrity should be investigated; and if he refuses to comply, his obstinacy will be clear, and he should be killed.[96] This is the meaning of *{clarify}*, meaning the problematic issue, or the variant reading *{ascertain}*, and do not be hasty: both have the same meaning. If anyone kills him without seeking clarification, he has committed a forbidden act. If someone says, "What about the Prophet's PBUH harshness towards Muhallim and the ejection of his corpse from the grave? How to explain that away? We say, "It is because the Prophet PBUH knew of his intention that he did not care about his Islam, but he had killed him deliberately due to a grievance that existed between them in the Age of Ignorance."

C13/10 Eighth, His Exalted word *{seeking temporal worldly gain}* meaning "desiring to seize his property." The wealth of this world is called 'temporal gain' because it is essentially transient, impermanent. Abu 'Ubayd said, "It is said that the whole of the wealth of this worldly life is *'arad* [i.e. temporal gain] – with a short *a* vowel above the letter *ra'* – and dirhams, hence the saying that "This world is temporal gain ready for the taking, from which both the righteous and the sinful eat." On the other hand, *'ard* [i.e. display] – with no vowel above the letter *ra'* – is everything other than dinars and dirhams. Thus, whilst every thing on display may be a temporal gain, not every temporal gain is on display. As recorded in *Sahih Muslim* from the Prophet PBUH, "Richness isn't from an

95 As opposed to *al-Salaam 'alaykum*.

96 The context here is obviously that of what we might today call a "border patrol force" coming across a suspicious, potentially armed stranger near the frontier with enemy territory. It does not obviously provide a justification to a "lone wolf terrorist", who has enjoyed living in safety in a community, to plot to kill indiscriminately members of that community if they don't first greet him or her on the street or in a shop with *al-Salaam 'alaykum*. Implied in what Imam al-Qurtubi wrote is the power to detain suspects, if necessary, in order to carry out any necessary investigation, something which has not been observed in those who plot to kill ordinary people travelling in buses, trains, civilian aircraft or wandering around in marketplaces.

abundance of worldly goods, rather richness is self-sufficiency."[97] A scholar took this meaning and versified it:

"Be satisfied with enough and be content.
"Do you know you'll live till dusk or dawn?
"Being rich isn't due to owing much, rather
"Being rich or poor comes from the soul."

This corrects what Abu 'Ubaydah said, "Wealth comprises all that makes one rich." In *Kitab al-'ayn*, the word *'arad* is whatever can be possessed of this world, as in (Q. 8:67) *{you want temporal worldly gain}*, [98] and its plural is *'urud*." In *al-Mujmal* by Ibn Faris, "The word *'arad* [in the sense of 'symptom'] is whatever befalls a human by way of illness of the like, and in the sense of 'temporal worldly gain' means whatever the world contains of wealth, be it little or much. In terms of chattels, *'arad* is everything other than money. A thing is said to be avoided if it appears and could have been taken. Also *'ard* [in the sense of 'breadth'] is the opposite of length."

C13/11 Nineth, His Exalted word *{Bounties aplenty exist with Allah}* is a promise from Allah the Exalted of what He will bring out of His own magnificence and generosity for not committing a forbidden act, meaning "Don't backslide." *{That is how you used to be before}* meaning that that is how you used to conceal your faith from your people, out of fear for your own safety, until Allah granted you the blessings of the strengthening of the religion and the overpowering of the associators. Now they are like that, every one of them amongst his people, waiting for his chance to reach you. It is not fitting therefore, when he reaches you, that you kill him until you are clear regarding him. Ibn Zayd said, "The meaning is

97 This hadith plays on the different connotations of the Arabic word *ghiná*, at the heart of which is the concept of not being dependent on others for anything, as God is Self-sufficient. Hence, in this life, whoever is rich in terms of worldly goods may be referred to as being "of independent means," not needing the material support of others.

98 The verse from which this phrase comes was revealed after the Battle of Badr (2 AH/624 CE) when, rather than focusing on the fight, some of the Muslim army chose to put their energies into capturing wealthy hostages whom they could later ransom, as had been the custom in pre-Islamic Arabia.

that that is how you were as disbelievers, *{until Allah favoured you}* by your accepting Islam. So, do not deny the possibility that he too is like that, and that he will then accept Islam in his own time when he meets you. Therefore you must ascertain his actual situation."

C13/12 Tenth, those who say that faith is solely based on utterance have used this verse as evidence due to His Exalted word *{and, when someone extends to you a greeting of peace, do not say, "You are not a believer,"}*. They say, "When He forbade it to be said to whoever says, 'There is no god but Allah,' 'You are not a believer', He also forbade killing them based solely on that statement. If it had not been for the evidence of faith, which is this statement, he would not have found fault in their statement." We replied, "Some people were only in doubt in case this statement of his was mere self-preservation, whereas Allah never required His servants to judge other than by what is apparent. Allah's Messenger PBUH said, "I was commanded to fight people until they say, 'There is no god but Allah.' There is nothing in that to suggest that faith is only a declaration. Have you not considered that the hypocrites used to say these words, but they were not believers according to what has been explained above in *Surat al-Baqarah*; and his PBUH statement on this has shed light on the explanation, 'Didn't you split his heart open?' where he established that faith is a declaration and something else. Its reality is acceptance by the heart, but God's servant has no way to establish the fact except what he hears from the other person." Those who say, "The repentance of a heretic is accepted if he manifests Islam," also use this as evidence, saying, "because Allah the Exalted does not distinguish between the heretic and others when he manifests Islam." Discussion of this topic has already occurred at the start of *Surat al-Baqarah*, including a rebuttal of the Qadariyah doctrine. Allah the Exalted informed us that He has favoured believers above all of creation by singling them out for success, whereas the Qadariyah sect says, "He created them all with faith." If it were as the Qadariyah sect claims, then there would be no meaning to singling out the believers from amongst all of creation by bestowing on them His favour.

C13/13 Eleventh, His Exalted saying *{So clarify}* repeats the command for clarification as confirmation that *{Allah is ever Aware of what you do}* to warn against going against Allah's command, meaning safeguard yourselves and keep away from an error that could lead you into peril.

Soundbite 14: "Regarding a *harbi kafir* who is killed by a Muslim..."

IMAM ABU HANIFA (R) SAID, "REGARDING A HARBI KAFIR WHO IS KILLED BY A MUSLIM, THERE IS NO RETALIATION (AGAINST THE KILLER) & THE DIYAH IS NOT TO BE PAID, BECAUSE THE BLOOD OF THE KAFIR IS HALAL (TO SHED) UNLESS IT IS ESTABLISHED THAT HE HAS A COVENANT OR IS UNDER DHIMMAH." -AL HAWI AL KABIR[99]

C14/1 al-Shafi'i said, "And a believer should not be killed in retribution for a disbeliever due to the Prophet's PBUH statement, 'A believer is not to be killed for a disbeliever.' There is no dispute that nor should he be killed in retribution for someone from enemy territory granted safe passage, who is similar to one protected by covenant in terms of the prohibition of killing him." al-Mazani – Allah have mercy on him – said, "If he is not to be killed in retribution for one type of disbeliever whose blood it is forbidden to shed, then he should not be killed for another type."

C14/2 al-Shafi'i – Allah have mercy on him – said, "Someone said that the Prophet PBUH meant thereby that a believer should not be killed in retribution for an enemy disbeliever. However, is there any clarification to corroborate a claim such as this? I replied, 'Yes! The statement of the Prophet PBUH that a believer does not inherit from a disbeliever, nor a disbeliever from a believer. So, do you claim that he intended only the disbelieving people of the land of war because shedding their blood and seizing their wealth are lawful?' He answered, 'No! Rather it refers to all disbelievers, as the label of disbelief applies to them all.' We said, 'And likewise, a believer is not to be killed in retribution for a disbeliever, as the label of disbelief applies to them all. So, where's the difference?' Someone said, 'We've narrated the hadith of 'Abd al-Rahman ibn

99 See https://shamela.ws/book/6157/5587 (viewed 27/05/2025) for the Arabic text of *Qala al-Shafi'i wa-la yuqtalu mu'min bi-kafir li-qawl al-Nabi* PBUH. This is a commentary by 'Ali ibn Muhammad al-Mawardi (d.450/1058) on *al-Mukhtaṣar min 'ilm al-Imām al-Nafīs Muḥammad ibn Idrīs*, a abridged work on Shafi'i law by Isma'il ibn Yahya al-Muzani (d.264/878). This soundbite begs a question: Why quote from a Shafi'i book that is seeking to demonstrate the relative weakness of Abu Hanifah's school's jurisprudential stance rather than from a Hanafi book to ensure that the Hanafi stance has not been misquoted, as here, and misrepresented?

al-Baylamani.'[100] We replied, "It has a broken chain of transmission and is therefore incorrect. According to what has reached us, it was narrated that 'Amr ibn Umayyah killed a disbeliever who had a pact of safety for period; so, the Prophet PBUH had 'Amr killed in retribution for the victim, who was an ambassador. Even if the account were established as true, I would rule against it, as it was abrogated because that disbeliever was killed some time before the Conquest of Mecca, while the command in Allah's Messenger's PBUH sermon that a believer is not to be killed for a disbeliever is from the year of the Conquest. Furthermore, it is factually incorrect because 'Amr ibn Umayyah was still alive some considerable time after the Prophet PBUH. You are taking knowledge second-hand from those who are distant. As a result, you do not have the expertise of our companions.'"

C14/3 Al-Mawardi said, "As for the rulings on equivalence regarding being free and a Muslim, for us consideration is given to retribution being by someone of higher social status against someone of lower social status and not the other way round. Hence a disbeliever is killed for a Muslim, but not a Muslim for a disbeliever, regardless of whether the disbeliever is a protected non-Muslim, is covered by covenant, or is hostile; and this is what Malik, Ahmad and Ishaq said, while Abu Hanifah said, '**A Muslim should be killed** in retribution **for a protected non-Muslim but not for** a disbeliever **covered by treaty, or an enemy disbeliever**.'[101] al-Sha'bi said, 'A Muslim should be killed in retribution for a Jew or Christian of the People of the Book but for not a Zoroastrian.'"

---

100 This refers to a weak hadith in al-Bayhaqi's *al-Khilafiyat*, that the Prophet PBUH reportedly took retribution against a Muslim for a non-Muslim protected by covenant, as mentioned below.

101 This is the closest match found in the text named to the soundbite listed by the Daesh propagandist, who translated it thus, "Regarding a *harbi kafir* [enemy disbeliever] who is killed by a Muslim, there is no retaliation (against the killer) and the *diyat* [blood money] is not to be paid, because the blood of the *kafir* is *halal* (to shed) unless it is established that he has a covenant or is under *dhimmah*," where *dhimmah* means the protected status granted to non-Muslim citizens of a Muslim-ruled state in return for payment of the *jizyah* tribute], as distinct from a disbeliever from enemy territory, such as a merchant, who is granted leave to enter Muslim territory under a covenant of safety. However, this is a misquotation of the Hanafi stance, which actually states that "a Muslim is to be killed in retribution for a protected non-Muslim citizen, but he is not to be killed for an enemy disbeliever granted safe passage ([*yuqtalu*] *al-Muslim bil-dhimmi wa-la yuqtalu bil-musta'min*)."

C14/4 They produced in evidence the general literal meaning of the statement of Allah, the Exalted (Q.5:45) *{& have prescribed for you in the Torah that a life for a life...}* and His saying (Q.2:179) *{& you have in retribution as a deterrent a protection of life}* as well as the narration of Ibn al-Baylamani that the Prophet PBUH had a Muslim slain for a disbeliever, saying, "I am the worthiest of all who are loyal to their covenant of protection." Also in what has been narrated that 'Amr ibn Umayyah al-Damri killed an associator, and so Allah's Messenger PBUH had him slain; and in what has been narrated that Abu Musa al-Ash'ari wrote to 'Umar ibn al-Khattab – may Allah be pleased with him – to ask him about the case of a Muslim who killed a Christian, and 'Umar wrote to him to exact retribution from him.

C14/5 From the perspective of analogy, whoever a disbeliever may be slain for, it is permissible to slay in retribution for a disbeliever, just like the disbeliever. Also, given that whoever may be slain in retribution for killing people of his own religion, it is permissible to slay him in retribution for someone not of his own religion, like slaying a Jew in retribution for a Christian; and given that a Muslim is forever on a level with the protected non-Muslim in terms of sparing their blood, then it is necessary to carry out retribution between them both just like between Muslims. Similarly, given that the sanctity of the life of a protected non-Muslim is far more inviolable than the sanctity of his property, and it has been established that the hand of a Muslim is to be amputated for stealing the property of a protected non-Muslim, so it is even more fitting that he should forfeit his hand in retribution for a protected non-Muslim's hand. Likewise, given that a disbeliever, if he were to kill another disbeliever and then to accept Islam, his Islam would not prevent the execution of retribution, so too it would not prevent the necessity of retribution.[102] Furthermore, since it is permitted for a disbeliever to kill a Muslim in self-defence, then retribution for his life has priority, and in both cases it involves slaying a Muslim for a disbeliever.[103]

---

102 This statement is interesting in the prison context, where some Muslim criminals express the view that the promise of converts not being held to account on Judgment Day for sins prior to conversion somehow implies that their imprisonment now is *de facto* oppression.

103 This final sentence of the paragraph seems to completely undermine the point intended by the Daesh propagandists who published the translated soundbite.

C14/6 Our evidence is His statement (Q.59:20) *{The denizens of the Fire and the denizens of Paradise are not equal}* so, the negation of equivalence between the two groups prevents the equivalence of their lives and the parity of their blood. If it is said, "One is not allowed to assign this Muslim to Paradise due the possibility of his later disbelieving; nor to assign a disbeliever to the Fire due to the possibility of his accepting Islam." It is said, "The ruling in the verse applies to the generality of the two types without being applied to particular individuals, even though the people of faith have been assigned Paradise, and the people of disbelief have been assigned the Fire. The Exalted has said (Q.4:141) *{Allah will never give the disbelievers a way to a conclusive victory over the believers}*; and even if this is expressed as a statement, the intended meaning is of prohibition. This is because a statement ought not to contradict the one making it; and yet we may see a disbeliever gain the upper hand over a Muslim. So, denying him a way to gain the upper hand prevents the need to retribution against him." If it is said, "It is predicated on his having no way to gain the upper hand over him in terms of argument and proof," on that there are two answers: first, that it is predicated on the generality taking into account the generality of the phrase; and second, that we know that he has no way to gain the upper hand over him on the basis of the indicative argument contained in this verse, so it is not permitted to predicate it on the basis of what is known from a source other than it.

C14/7 What also indicates this from the Sunnah, which is what is relied upon in the matter, is what Abu Hurayrah narrated and 'Imran ibn al-Husayn that the Prophet PBUH said, "A believer is not to be killed in retribution for a disbeliever." Ma'qil ibn Yasar also narrated that the Prophet PBUH said, "A believer is not to be killed in retribution for a disbeliever, nor is anyone with a valid covenant to be killed in retribution for a disbeliever." Qatadah narrated from al-Hasan, from Qays, who said, "I set off, me and al-Ashtar, to 'Ali ibn Abi Talib – Allah's pleasure be upon him – and said to him, 'Did Allah's Messenger PBUH commit you to anything that he did not commit people to generally?' 'Ali replied, 'No! except what is in this document.' Then he took a document out of the scabbard of his sword; and in it was written that the blood of Muslims is of equal worth; that they are as one hand against all others; that the right to grant protection extends to the least of them; and that a believer is not to be killed in retribution for a disbeliever, nor is anyone with a valid covenant.'" Hammad narrated from Jabir, from al-Sha'bi, from 'Ali ibn al-Husayn, who said, "My father brought out the sword of Allah's Messenger PBUH, and in it was written the terms of blood money is due from believers in general; that no one should be left isolated[104] in Islam; that a Muslim should not be killed in retribution for a disbeliever; that the isolated person who has no tribe[105] should join one; and he PBUH commanded that he should be joined to a tribe and added to it so that he would not be alone. So, all these texts indicate that a Muslim should not be killed in retribution for a disbeliever.

C14/8 If they say, "The intention behind his PBUH saying, 'A Muslim should not be killed in retribution for a disbeliever' means specifically the enemy disbeliever because he PBUH also said, 'nor anyone with a valid covenant,' whereas a disbeliever with a covenant may be killed in retribution for another disbeliever with a covenant but not for an enemy disbeliever, since the ruling with a grammatical conjunction agrees with the ruling for that which is conjoined to it," on this there are two responses. First, that his PBUH saying, 'A Muslim should not be killed in retribution for a disbeliever' covers the entirety of disbelievers, be they covered by a covenant or from an enemy population. So, it must be applied to the entirety of disbelievers; nor is it permissible to restrict its meaning by suppressing a fact or interpretation. As for his PBUH saying, 'nor anyone with a valid covenant,' it is grammatically a subject meaning that, because of his covenant of safety, anyone with a valid covenant should not be

104 The word 'isolated' here refers either to a person whose dead body is found abandoned in the desert, or possibly someone unable to pay the blood money for an accidental homicide from his or her own resources. In either case, the Sharia requires that the Muslim community – or the state – assume the cost of compensating the deceased's next of kin, if there is no tribe to raise the necessary funds for the blood money.

105 So, for example, non-Arabs entering into Islam in the early days would become clients – or affiliated members – of an Arab tribe that had already accepted Islam.

killed,[106] and that a covenant on his part guarantees the sparing the shedding of the blood of covenant holders. The second response is that his PBUH saying, 'A Muslim should not be killed in retribution for a disbeliever' is to be taken generally for every disbeliever, whether he has a covenant of safety or is an enemy combatant, while 'nor anyone with a valid covenant' is to be taken as specific, in that he is not to be killed in retribution for an enemy disbeliever, even if the latter is killed by non-Muslim with a covenant because the specifying of either one of the two aforementioned does not require the specification of the other.

C14/9 What was narrated from Prophet PBUH also indicates that, that he said, "If I were ever to have killed a Muslim for a disbeliever in retribution, I would have killed Khidam for al-Hudhali." If it had been permitted to kill Khidam for some categories of disbelievers but not others and not to have released him, he PBUH would have done so. What indicates that is the form of the expression that a Muslim, since he is not to be killed in retribution for an enemy disbeliever granted safe passage, is not to be killed for a protected non-Muslim. As for joining the two together, there are three reasons.

C14/10 First, the protected non-Muslim's claim is nullified due to his disbelief; so, if a Muslim kills him, there must be no retribution for him, the same as for an enemy disbeliever granted safe passage.

C14/11 The second reason is that whoever is immune from enslavement due to his religion is not to be killed in retribution for whoever is not immune from enslavement due to his religion, just like an enemy disbeliever granted safe passage. If it is argued that this contradicts the case of a disbeliever, if he kills another disbeliever, and then the killer accepts Islam, he is nonetheless to be killed in retribution for him, even though he has become a Muslim; on that there are two answers. One of them is that a condition of the reason is if a Muslim killed him, but in the example this man killed him when he was a

106 In other words, the point being made here is that if a non-Muslim with a covenant of safety kills a non-Muslim without such a covenant, a judge should not grant the latter's next of kin the right to shed the blood of the former in retribution.

disbeliever, so it does not contradict the reason. Second, the argument is based on the victim's category, so it is only contradicted by its equivalent. If it is argued that an enemy disbeliever granted safe passage lacks full inviolability because his blood is only spared for a given period, unlike a protected non-Muslim citizen, who enjoys total inviolability, as his blood spared in perpetuity, similar to a Muslim; on that there are two answers. One of them is that the difference in the two inviolability types in terms of duration does not prevent the equivalence of both in terms of ruling despite the duration of the period. Do you not consider that the prohibition on sexual intercourse with an unrelated woman is temporary while the prohibition on sexual intercourse with a woman within the prohibited degrees of marriage is perpetual, yet they are equal in terms of having to execute the prescribed penalty for fornication? Likewise in this instance. The second response is that for the taking of a life, there are two alternatives: retribution and blood money. Given that their difference in inviolability does not prevent their equivalence in terms of blood money, nor does it prevent their equivalence in terms of retribution. Likewise, breaching the inviolability of a person's honour necessitates the prescribed penalty for slander, and breaching the inviolability of a person's life necessitates retribution. Moreover, given that the prescribed penalty for slander is quashed for the Muslim who insults a non-Muslim, how much more appropriate is it that retribution should be quashed in respect of his life, since taking a life in retribution is far harsher than exacting the prescribed penalty for slander? As for responding to His Exalted saying (Q.5:45) *{&, concerning it, We decreed for them that there should be a life for a life}* it has two facets. First, it refers back to the Israelites, who were all equal; so, it is not permissible to apply their ruling on those who are unequal. Second, it is a generality particularised on the basis of evidence. As for His Exalted saying (Q.2:179) *{& you have, in the principle of retribution, life}* it is that retribution is for them to take, but it is not permissible to exact retribution from them. As for the hadith of 'Abd al-Rahman ibn al-Baylamani that the Prophet PBUH killed a Muslim in retribution for a disbeliever, it is a weak hadith whose soundness hadith specialists have not established. Moreover, its transmission is incomplete, since Ibn al-Baylamani was not a companion of the Prophet PBUH; and, for us, incomplete transmissions are not a proof. Even if one accepted arguing on the basis of that hadith, it would not be evidence because a particular case does not set a general precedent. It may be that the killer accepted Islam after killing his victim, and so he PBUH had him killed in retribution for the victim. If one accepts this possibility, one must hold back from arguing on that basis.

C14/12 The third reason is that, in their narration, it is reported that the one whom he killed was an envoy granted safe passage. However, according to them, a Muslim is not to be killed in retribution for an enemy disbeliever granted safe passage. So, it is not evidence in their favour.

C14/13 As for the hadith of 'Umar, it has been narrated that Mu'adh ibn Jabal contested it. Instead, Mu'adh narrated to 'Umar from the Prophet PBUH that he said, "A Muslim should not be killed in retribution for a disbeliever," and that Zayd ibn said, "Don't kill your brother in retribution for your slave," so 'Umar retreated from his former stance and wrote to Abu Musa, "Don't kill him in retribution for the other," and that became a consensus.[107] As for their analogy of the Muslim, its meaning is that the shedding of his blood was spared because of his religion, and also that his religion prevents his being enslaved, unlike a disbeliever. as for their analogy of the killing of a Jew by a Christian, it is incorrect because, in our opinion, all disbelief is effectively a single denomination, even if it varies. So, for that reason, killing in retribution is upheld between them; whereas the faith of Islam is different from both Judaism and Christianity, and it has precedence over them.

C14/14 As for the hadith of 'Amr ibn Umayyah al-Damri, al-Shafi'i responded to it in three ways. First, that the way it is transmitted is weak, its narrators being unknown. Second, that 'Amr ibn Umayyah al-Damri survived the Prophet PBUH and died during the time of Mu'awiyah, so what has been attributed to him is impossible. For that reason, al-Shafi'i said, "You take information second-hand from a distance. As a result, you do not have

107 This refers back to para. C14/4 above.

the expertise of our companions," meaning the people of the two sacred mosques in Mecca and Medina, because Allah's Messenger PBUH lived amongst them, and they were more knowledgeable about what he said and about his companions."

C14/15 They state that breaching the inviolability of a life is far harsher than breaching the inviolability of property, and that a Muslim's hand may be amputated for stealing a disbeliever's property. So it is more fitting that he be killed in retribution for the life of a disbeliever. The response to that has two facets. First, amputation in cases of stealing is a right of Allah the Exalted, the pardoning of which is not permitted, so it is deserved in the case of a disbeliever's property as in the case of a Muslim's property. However, killing in retribution is one of the rights of humans since it may be pardoned; so, a disbeliever does not deserve it over a Muslim. Second, just as it is permissible to amputate a Muslim's hand for stealing the property of an enemy disbeliever granted safe passage, though he may not be killed in retribution for him, amputation is also permissible for stealing the property of a protected non-Muslim citizen, even if it is an insignificant amount. They are analogous to the disbeliever, meaning that they are both equal in terms of the status of their religion.

C14/16 They state that a disbeliever should be killed in retribution for a disbeliever, even if he accepts Islam after killing his victim; and likewise if he was a Muslim before he killed him. This has no basis because killing in retribution is a prescribed penalty, and prescribed penalties are taken as arising from the circumstance of the necessity of their application, not of what occurred after it. Hence, if an insane person kills and then regains his senses, killing in retribution does not apply to him; whereas if he was sane at the time of killing and then becomes insane, killing in retribution would apply to him. Al-Awza'i took the view that a person should not be killed in retribution if he accepts Islam, holding to the literal meaning of his PBUH saying, "A Muslim should not be killed in retribution for a disbeliever," even though we differed with him over it based on the meaning that we mentioned above.

C14/17 They state that, since it is permissible for a non-Muslim[108] to kill a Muslim in self-defence, it is permissible for a non-Muslim to kill a Muslim in retribution. This can be interpreted in two ways. First, it is permitted for an enemy disbeliever granted safe passage to kill a Muslim in self-defence, and it is not permitted to kill that non-Muslim in retribution for his Muslim victim. Second, in relation to property, it is permitted to kill a Muslim while repelling him from it, but he is not to be killed in order to acquire it.[109]

C14/18 What prevents discussing and acting on the killing of a Muslim in retribution for a disbeliever, since souls recoil at the mere thought of it.

C14/19 Yahya ibn Zakariya al-Saji related from Musa ibn Ishaq al-Ansari, from 'Ali ibn 'Amr al-Ansari that the case of a Muslim who had killed a disbeliever was brought before Abu Yusuf,[110] the cadi, and he ruled that retribution should be exacted against him. A man came to him with a scrap of parchment from a Baghdadi poet known as Abu al-Mudarriji, on which was written the lines:

O killer of a Muslim for a disbeliever,
You are wrong. The just is unlike the oppressor.
O whoever is of Baghdad and its environs,
Among the people's jurists or a poet,
Abu Yusuf has gone against the religion
By slaying a Muslim for a disbeliever.
Reflect and weep for your religion, and
Show patience, for patience is rewarded.

Abu Yusuf took the parchment and sought an audience with the Caliph Harun al-Rashid, where he told him the situation and read out to him the

108 From the context, this right extends only to non-Muslim citizens or to those who have entered Muslim territory legally, not to marauding enemy disbelievers.

109 The last five Arabic words appear to mean that, while it is lawful to kill a fellow Muslim in defence of one's property during an act of robbery, for example, it is unlawful to hunt down and kill him to retrieve it. In the latter case, it is for a judge to decide.

110 Abu Yusuf (d.182/798) was a prominent student of Abu Hanifah, and he was appointed cadi, or judge, by the Abbasid caliph, Harun al-Rashid. In this anecdote, fear of public outcry prevented Abu Yusuf's attempt to execute a judgement based on Hanafi jurisprudence.

contents of the parchment. So, al-Rashid told him, "Handle this matter with cunning to avoid strife arising out of it." So, Abu Yusuf left and requested of the victim's next of kin clear proof that he had truly been a protected person and had paid the *jizyah* tribute. When they could not produce it, he annulled the retribution ruling, commuting it to a ruling of compensation with blood money. This is how to deal with such a case if it could lead to disapproval and the spread of disturbances of the peace, then it is more fitting and proper to forgo execution.

Soundbite 15: "There is no expiation, no blood money paid for killing a *kafir*..."

IBN MUFLIH (R) SAID, "THERE IS NO EXPIATION, NO BLOOD MONEY PAID FOR KILLING A KAFIR THAT HAS NO PEACE TREATY, BECAUSE HIS BLOOD IS GENERALLY HALAL (TO SPILL) LIKE THE PIG."-AL MUBDI[111]

C15/1 *"Chapter on the conditions of retribution, which are four* in number,*"*[112] as the author will mention.

C15/2 *"First, that the criminal be of sound mind,"* as retribution is a form of punishment, whereas it is inappropriate for whoever lacks mental capacity. *"As for the child and the lunatic, there is no retribution against either of them"* without dispute, because mental capacity is one of its conditions, and it is lacking in them. It is likewise if there is temporary impairment of mental capacity for an excusable reason, such as sleeping, loss of consciousness, as there is no valid intention in such people. If someone were to say, "On the day of the killing, I was a minor or mad," he should be believed with the possibility of swearing a solemn oath. However, if he falsely says, "I am now a minor, so there should be no retribution or swearing an oath," or in the case of the drunk and the like whose mental capacity is impaired for an inexcusable reason, like the one who consumes narcotic drugs, *"there are two* relevant *narrations."* Abu al-Khattab mentioned that that was based on his divorce,[113] and on that too there are two narrations. On the requirement of retribution against him, there are two opinions: first, that it is not required due to

111 See https://shamela.ws/book/21619/2864 (viewed 27/05/2025) for the Arabic text of *Bab shurut al-qisas wa-hiya arba'ah* in this commentary on a manual of Hanbali law, the full title of which is *al-Mubdi' fi sharh al-Muqni'*.

112 Only the first two conditions for valid retribution (*qisas*) appear in this excerpt: first, that the criminal be of sound mind; and second, that is retribution be taken from someone who is otherwise immune from harm (i.e. not an outlaw). The other two are: "Third, that the victim be socially equivalent to the perpetrator" and "Fourth, is that the killer be not the father of the victim." In other words, instead of finding a source that deals explicitly with the laws of war, what the Daesh propagandists did was take out of context a scholarly mediaeval explanation of whether the principle of "an eye for an eye", etc., applies in relation to those found guilty of murder or culpable homicide.

113 This reference to Abu al-Khattab is by way of analogy on the making of a false statement to avoid the consequence of one's actions, as becomes clearer below in this paragraph.

temporary loss of mental capacity, as with madness, and that he lacks capacity like a child. *"The more valid of the two is that retribution is required,"* which Ibn Qudamah supported in *al-Mughni* and its commentary, while al-Qadi and the author of *al-Wajiz*[114] were clear-cut about it on the grounds that the Companions mandated the prescribed penalty for slander on Abu al-Khattab.[115] If the prescribed penalty for slander was required in that case, then a clear case of retribution is a human right which is more deserving; also because there is scope for his defiance becoming a reason for the penalty being dropped, whereas divorce is a statement that can be declared void, unlike killing.

C15/3 Section: *"The second condition is that the one killed be immune,"* meaning that he is immune from the shedding of his blood,[116] because retribution was only legislated to preserve the blood of those immune from being shed, and to prevent the ruin of the society's foundations whose continued survival is sought; and that is lacking in those criminals and others who are not legally immune.[117]

C15/4 *"So, retribution is not required for killing an enemy disbeliever."* We know of no dispute in this. **Neither is blood money required for killing him, nor atonement, because shedding his blood is permitted without**

114 This is *al-Wajiz fi al-fiqh 'ala madhhab al-Imam Ahmad ibn Hanbal* by al-Husayn ibn Yusuf al-Dujayli (d.732/1331), a contemporary of Ibn Muflih, the author of this excerpt.

115 A similar instance occurred during the lifetime of the Prophet PBUH, as reported in *Sahih al-Bukhari* and elsewhere, when Hilal ibn Umayyah accused his wife of adultery with Sharik ibn Sahmah, and the Prophet PBUH ordered that he be flogged for slander unless he produced the proof required (Q.24:4), namely the testimony of four witnesses of good character.

116 This refers to the authentic saying of the Prophet PBUH recorded in *Sahih al-Bukhari* (no. 6878) and elsewhere that it is not lawful to shed the blood of any Muslim who has testified that there is no god but Allah and that Muhammad is His Messenger except for one of three reasons: a life for a life; the married fornicator; and the one who emerges from the religion and abandons the body of believers.

117 Neither the Prophet PBUH nor his companions, nor the serious Islamic scholars who followed them have ever advocated Muslims taking the law into their own hands, as was the custom in pre-Islamic Arabian society. As recorded in al-Nawawi's collection of forty hadiths, drawing on *Sahih al-Bukhari, Sahih Muslim, Jami' al-Tirmidhi, Sunan al-Bayhaqi* and other sources, Ibn 'Abbas reported that the Prophet PBUH said, "If people were given whatever they claimed, then men would claim other people's property and their blood. However, evidence is required of the plaintiff, and a solemn oath from the defendant."

restriction as with the killing of **swine,**[118] and because Allah the Exalted commanded his killing, saying (Q.9:5) *{So, slay the associators}*, regardless of whether the killer was a Muslim or a protected non-Muslim; *"nor an apostate,"* because shedding his blood is permitted, just like that of the enemy disbeliever; *"nor a married fornicator,"* meaning that neither retribution, nor blood money, nor atonement is required for killing him, just as with the apostate. Some have expressed an opinion that retaliation falls on his clan because executing his killing should be referred to the ruler, as in the case of the one against whom retribution is due, if someone who had no right were to kill him. The response to that he is someone whose blood it is permitted to shed, and whose killing is imperative; so, like the enemy disbeliever, he is not guaranteed safety. The apparent meaning is "even if it is before producing him before a ruler," Ibn Muflih said in *al-Ri'ayah* and *al-Furu'*,[119] "and the intended meaning is before repentance," hence the blood is shed with impunity; or after it, if his repentance is accepted at face value, as in the case of a sudden acceptance of Islam. It indicates that the outcome for a married fornicator is effectively like an apostate, especially since their utterance is like an organ of a soul whose killing is required,[120] but may receive a discretionary punishment for usurping the right of the legal authority, as

118 This has been translated by the Daesh propagandists as "There is no expiation, no blood money paid for killing a kafir that has no peace treaty, because his blood is generally halal (to spill) like the pig." It is not a throwaway insult by the author, Ibn Muflih, nor is it general to any disbeliever who is 'hostile' to Islam in a metaphorical sense, but it relates specifically to enemy disbelievers killed at a time of war, as becomes clear when compared with the *Chapter on dividing spoils of war* (*Bab qismat al-ghana'im*) from elsewhere in *al-Mubdi'*:

"*'Spoils are all property taken from the associators by force in battle.'* His saying *'all property'* includes whatever makes one wealthy, such as a crucifix, which are to be broken, while pigs are to be killed. Ahmad ibn Hanbal said it, and Abu Dawud transmitted: *'He should pour out wine but not break the containers.'* As for dogs, they are not included in the spoils, and it is for the ruler to assign them to whomever he wishes. His saying *'from the associators'* means the belligerents; and his saying *'by force in battle'*, this relates to a portion out of which comes the tribute."

119 *Kitab al-furu'* is a work by Ibn Muflih on the branches of Hanbali law. As for *al-Ri'ayah*, this may be a reference to either *al-Ri'ayah al-kubra* or *al-Ri'ayah al-sughra* by another Hanbali scholar, Ahmad ibn Hamdan, known as Ibn Hamdan (d.695/1295).

120 The concept behind this is complicated, but it may refer to the fact that the penalty for adultery can under certain circumstances be warded off by a denial under oath, and that liability for the penalty for apostasy likewise is often the result of something said by the accused, which can be

with the one who kills an enemy disbeliever. *"& if the killer is a protected non-Muslim"* there is a caution over the legal equivalence of the protected non-Muslim to the Muslim in that regard, because from either of them the killing hits the mark, and it may be tolerated in the case where a protected non-Muslim kills a married Muslim fornicator. The author of *al-Targhib* said it because executing a prescribed penalty is our right, as Muslims, and the ruler is the designated authority. In *al-Rawdah*, he said that if the victim's attorney or a stranger pre-emptively kills a highwayman before he arrives in front of the ruler, there is no retaliation, because his blood has been shed with impunity, so – according to its apparent meaning – there is no blood money.

C15/5 However, it is not so *"if a Muslim or a protected non-Muslim were to cut off the hand of an apostate or an enemy disbeliever who accepted Islam and later died; or who shot an enemy disbeliever who accepted Islam before the arrow brought him down. In that case, nothing is held against the killer."* That is because he did not harm anyone who had immunity from the shedding of his blood at the time of shooting; and because he shot someone whom he had the authority to shoot. So, the victim does not enjoy a guarantee of safety because, in assigning a guarantee, consideration is given to the situation that exists at the start of life, because it alone is of binding relevance; and not every enemy disbeliever or apostate deserves a guarantee of safety. Therefore the perpetrator has no case to answer for the lapsing of the conditional eligibility for any guarantee of safety to be due.[121] Its apparent meaning is that no retribution or blood money is due from him. In *al-Targhib*, he has been

warded off by his or her renewal of acceptance of Islam. In both cases, an utterance can secure the accused's immunity from the lawful execution of punishment. But God knows best.

121 This is a bit convoluted, but essentially it appears to mean that if an enemy disbeliever or an apostate dies from an arrow shot by a Muslim or a protected non-Muslim but, between being shot at and dying, the victim converts or returns to Islam, then the archer is not liable to compensate or atone for the death because, at the time the arrow was shot, the victim was a lawful target. To understand this legal point, it may help to consider an opposite situation from a hadith in *Sahih al-Bukhari* where, in a battle against the hostile Juhaynah tribe, the companion Usamah ibn Zayd ignores a fallen man's declaration of faith, and instead thrusts his spear into him and kills him. When the Prophet [PBUH] heard this, he asked Usamah repeatedly, "Did you kill him after he had said, 'There is no god but Allah'?"

likened to someone who accepts Islam before being struck as, for example, if he shoots an apostate who accepts Islam before the arrow hits him, then there is no retribution because he shot at someone who had no immunity from shedding his blood, just like the enemy disbeliever. *"& regarding blood money, there are two opinions."* One of them is that it is not required, which is the better-known view, as with the apostasy of a Muslim and with an enemy disbeliever; and second, that it is required because shooting here is forbidden because of what it entails regarding usurping the right of the ruler, like his destroying a well that has been dug. It is also said that it is like in the case of the apostate, due to his negligence, since killing the apostate was not his duty. According to al-Hulwani,[122] practice is based on the first opinion.

122 Abu Muhammad 'Abd al-Rahman ibn Muhammad al-Hulwani, known as Ibn Abi al-Fath (d.546/1151).

Soundbite 16: "Shedding his blood is halal without exception, just like swine."

IBN QUDAMAH (R) SAID ABOUT THE HARBI KAFIR, "SHEDDING HIS BLOOD IS HALAL WITHOUT EXCEPTION, JUST LIKE SWINE." -AL MUGHNI[123]

C16/1 Section: "And a protected non-Muslim is not to be killed for a hostile disbeliever."[124] We know of no dispute on this, as shedding his blood is halal without exception, just like swine;[125] nor is there any blood money or atonement[126] for that. Nor is retribution, blood money or atonement required in the killing of an apostate, regardless of whether the one who killed him was a Muslim or a protected non-Muslim. This above is the opinion of some of al-Shafi'i's followers. Others among al-Shafi'i's followers stated that retribution was required of a protected non-Muslim who killed an apostate, or blood money if he was pardoned retribution,

123 See https://shamela.ws/book/8463/3653 (viewed 27/05/2025) for the Arabic text of *Fasl wa-la yuqtalu dhimmi bi-harbi*.

124 The point that Ibn Qudamah is making in his commentary relates to this first sentence, which shows that the life of a protected non-Muslim is not to be forfeit if he slays a hostile disbeliever. In other words, it is only a particular category of non-Muslim that has no right to demand retribution or compensation. It is certainly not evidence of a scholar-endorsed licence for Muslims to go out and kill non-Muslims indiscriminately.

125 Or, "the shedding of the hostile disbeliever's blood is permitted without restriction, just like a pig's." Reading this in context only goes to show the dangers of the extremist non-holistic, highlighter-pen approach to scholarship, as found in many damaged Islamic books in prison faith libraries. Elsewhere Ibn Qudamah in *al-Mughni* writes on the issue of damage to wine or swine belonging to a protected non-Muslim:

> "Issue: He said, 'Whoever damages the wine or swine of a protected non-Muslim has no fine to pay, and it is prohibited to interfere in whatever of their affairs they do not openly display.' The general meaning of that is that there is no liability regarding wine and pigs, whether the one causing the damage was a Muslim or a protected non-Muslim to a protected non-Muslim or a Muslim. Ahmad ibn Hanbal declared that, in the account of Abu al-Harith regarding a man who spilled the alcohol of a Muslim or the wine of a protected non-Muslim, that there is no liability. Al-Shafi'i said likewise. Abu Hanifah and Malik said that liability exists, if is it a protected non-Muslim who incurs a loss."

In other words, one cannot enter a non-Muslim's home to search for and spill their wine.

126 Atonement in the form of freeing a slave or – if unable to do that – fasting non-stop for two consecutive months is mentioned in the Qur'an (Q.4:92) in relation to a Muslim who unintentionally kills a believer from a hostile people or of a member of a people with whom the Muslims have a treaty or covenant.

because there is no lawful power of attorney in relation to his killing. Yet others have said that retribution is required, not blood money, because he has no value. According to us,[127] shedding the blood of an apostate is allowed, just like that of an hostile disbeliever; and that is because whoever's safety a Muslim does not guarantee, a protected non-Muslim does not guarantee it either, as with the hostile disbeliever.

127 In other words, the decontextualised soundbite is not the view of Ibn Qudamah, as propagandists indicate, but that of some unnamed members of the Shafi'i school.

Soundbite 17: "& it is halal to kill anyone other than those mentioned..."

IBN HAZM (R) SAID, "& IT IS HALAL TO KILL ANYONE OTHER THAN THOSE MENTIONED (WOMEN & KIDS) OF THE MUSHRIKEEN, BOTH THE COMBATANT & NON-COMBATANT, THE BUSINESSMAN & THE EMPLOYED, THE ELDERLY MAN WHETHER OR NOT HE IS A PERSON OF INFLUENCE, THE FARMER, THE BISHOP OR PRIEST OR MONK, THE BLIND OF CRIPPLE, NO ONE IS GIVEN EXCEPTION." -AL MUHALLA[128]

C17/1 Issue:[129] & killing their womenfolk is not lawful, nor the killing of those amongst them who have not reached puberty, except if any of those whom we have mentioned engages in fighting, and there is no other means of escape from them for the Muslim except by killing them, then at that point he has the right to kill them. It has been narrated to us through al-Bukhari, "Ahmad ibn Yunus told us, al-Layth – who is Ibn Sa'd – told us from Nafi' that Ibn 'Umar informed him that, in some of the Prophet's PBUH raids, a woman would be found killed, so Allah's Messenger PBUH disapproved of the killing of women and children."

C17/2 Issue: If, without being targeted, women and children are harmed in a night attack or are caught up in the fray, then there is no sin in that. It has been narrated to us through al-Bukhari, "'Ali ibn 'Abd Allah told us, Sufyan told us, al-Zuhri told us from 'Ubayd Allah ibn 'Abd Allah ibn 'Utbah, from Ibn 'Abbas, from al-Sa'b ibn Jaththamah al-Laythi, that Allah's Messenger PBUH was asked about the people of a settlement of associators who are attacked at night, and some of their women and offspring are harmed. He PBUH replied, 'They are from their fathers.'"[130]

---

128 See https://shamela.ws/book/767/2044 (viewed 27/05/2025) for the Arabic text of *Mas'alah wa-la yuhillu qatl man lam yablugh minhum* from *al-Muhallá bil-athar* by the Andalusian Zahiri scholar, Ibn Hazm (d.456/1064).

129 This first issue is numbered 926 in Ibn Hazm's work, and the next two follow on in order.

130 As a literalist, Ibn Hazm would have agreed that "They are from their fathers" is neither a command nor a licence to kill, but rather an acknowledgement that sometimes non-combatants are killed in battle.

C17/3 Issue: & it is halal [sic][131] to kill anyone other than those mentioned (women & kids) of the *mushrikeen*, both the combatant and non-combatant, the businessman and the employed, the elderly man whether or not he is a person of influence, the farmer, the bishop or priest or monk, the blind or cripple; no one is given exception.[132] It is also permitted to let them live. Allah the Exalted has said (Q.9:5) *{So, slay the associators wherever you find them, seize them, besiege them, and lie in wait in every place of ambush. However, if they repent, perform the prayer, and give zakat, let them go their way.}* He Who is Mighty and Majestic made killing general for all associators unless they accept Islam.[133]

C17/4 People have said, "None of those we have mentioned should be killed," and have argued on the basis of a tradition that we have narrated by way of Ahmad ibn Shu'ayb, whom Qutaybah informed, whom al-Mughirah informed from Abu al-Zinnad, from al-Muraqqa', from his grandfather Rabah ibn al-Rabi', who said, "We were with Allah's Messenger PBUH when he said to a man, 'Catch up with Khalid and tell him not to kill children or bondsmen.'" Also by way of Sufyan, from 'Abd Allah ibn Dhakwan, from al-Muraqqa' ibn Sayfi, from his uncle Hanzalah, the scribe, that Allah's Messenger PBUH said, "Do not kill children or bondsmen." Also by way of Abu Bakr ibn Abi Shaybah, whom Yahya ibn Adam informed, whom al-Hasan ibn Salih ibn Huyayy informed, from Khalid ibn al-Firz, from Anas ibn Malik, that Allah's Messenger PBUH said, "Set off in the name of Allah, and in the way of Allah, to fight the enemy of Allah; but do not kill frail old men, children or women." Also by way of Ibn Abi Shaybah, whom Humayd informed, from an old man of Medina who was the freed slave of Banu 'Abd al-Ashhal, from Dawud ibn al-Husayn, from 'Ikrimah, from Ibn 'Abbas that, when he dispatched his armies, Allah's Messenger PBUH used to say, "Don't kill the residents of monasteries." Also by way of

131 The English word 'permitted' or 'permissible' better reflects Ibn Hazm's choice of term (*ja'iz*) that the Daesh propagandist translated as 'halal' or 'lawful'.

132 The following is more accurate: "& it is permissible to kill any of the associators except those whom we have mentioned, combatants or non-combatants; merchants or employees, meaning a day worker; elderly men, whether their opinions on war are sought or not; peasants; bishops, priests or monks; the blind or crippled. Spare no one."

133 Ibn Hazm's Zahiri affiliation helps to explain why he adopted absolutely literal interpretations of the quotations that he selects from the Qur'an and Sunnah, as seen in this excerpt, thereby contradicting on occasions like this the majority of Sunni scholars.

al-Qa'nabi, whom Ibrahim ibn Isma'il informed, from Dawud ibn al-Husayn, from 'Ikrimah that Allah's Messenger PBUH said, "Don't kill the residents of monasteries." Also by way of Hammad ibn Salamah, whom 'Ubayd Allah ibn 'Umar informed, saying that 'Umar ibn 'Abd al-'Aziz wrote to some of his commanders that Allah's Messenger PBUH had said, "Don't kill small children, women, or elderly men." And from Hammad ibn Salamah, from an old man at Mina, from his father, that Allah's Messenger PBUH prohibited the killing of bondsmen and servants. Also by way of Qays ibn al-Rabi', from 'Umar the freed slave of 'Anbasah, from Zayd ibn 'Ali ibn al-Husayn, from his father, from 'Ali ibn Abi Talib, from the Prophet PBUH, who forbade the killing of old men or the chopping down of trees, unless the trees were harmful to them. Also by way of Ibn Abi Shaybah, from 'Isa ibn Yunus, from al-Ahwas, from Rashid ibn Sa'd, that the Prophet PBUH forbade the killing of old men who are not mobile. They also mentioned that Abu Bakr – may Allah be pleased with him – said to a commander of his, "You must not kill women, boys or frail old men. You will pass by people who have confined themselves to monasteries, they claim, for the sake of Allah. Call them to Islam and to Whom they have confined themselves for. You will also pass by people who have made the middle of their heads like nests, leaving their hair like headbands.[134] Strike with the sword where they have shaved their heads." From Jabir ibn 'Abd Allah, who said, "They would not kill the merchants of the associators, but would say, 'We only kill those who fight, and these don't fight.'"

C17/5 This is the entirety of what they have dragged up, and none of it is authentic.[135] As for al-Muraqqa's hadith, al-Muraqqa' is unknown.[136] As for the hadith of Ibn 'Abbas, it is from an unnamed old man of Medina,

134 i.e. the tonsure of certain Christian monastic and priestly orders.

135 To discredit those who criticise his argument on the lawfulness of slaying any adult male, what Ibn Hazm appears – perhaps disingenuously – to have done above is to have chosen to attribute to his opponents only those narrations that contain some demonstrable flaw in their chains of transmission and then, as here, to enumerate those flaws, disregarding the fact that other sound narrations of those hadiths exist, which contradict his stance. The https://dorar.net website has been used to check the authenticity of any other narrations of the hadiths quoted by Ibn Hazm in this excerpt from *al-Muhalla*.

136 This first hadith appears only to have been recorded by Ibn Hazm.

though some have named him as Ibrahim ibn Isma'il ibn Abi Habibah, who is weak in transmission.[137] The other two accounts are incomplete in chain of transmission. Likewise, the hadith of Rashid is incomplete in chain of transmission, and incompletely transmitted hadiths are not proof. As for the hadith of Anas, it is from Khalid ibn al-Firz, who is unknown.[138] The hadith of Hammad ibn Salamah is from an old man of Mina, from his father; and this is very odd,[139] and what is ever odder than that is that a verse of the Qur'an is abandoned in favour of that. As for the hadith of Qays ibn al-Rabi', Qays is not strong as a transmitter, nor is 'Umar the freed slave of 'Anbasah known; while 'Ali ibn al-Husayn was only born after the death of his grandfather – may Allah be pleased with them both – so whatever they have misattributed to him falls. As for the narration from Abu Bakr, amongst their peculiarities is this particular tradition from Abu Bakr – may Allah be pleased with him – in which comes the assertion that Abu Bakr – may Allah be pleased with him – forbade the wounding of any camel or sheep except if it was to be eaten. Also coming in that tradition on Abu Bakr is that one should not cut down trees or drown beehives, whereas they have gone against him as they wish even where it is lawful to oppose it, since the Sunnah concurs with it, and where no practice contrary to it is known from the Companions. They then argue on the strength of it on points where others of the Companions – may Allah be pleased with them – took contrary positions, which is especially odd in relation to a single tradition.

C17/6 As for Jabir's saying that they did not used to kill merchants from among the associators, they have no evidence of that in that tradition because he did not say that they withheld from killing them in the land of war, but only informed about their orders in general terms. Furthermore, even if it is correct, clarifying therefrom, they still have no connexion in it to a command, since it contains no prohibition on killing non-Muslim

137 Two other narrations survive, one from Rabah ibn al-Rabi', classed as authentic, and another from Jamilah bint Sa'd ibn al-Rabi', classed as sound.
138 Ibn Hazm quoted this from *Sunan Abi Dawud*, and al-Albani too has classed it as weak.
139 There is another narration from 'Abd Allah ibn 'Umar that is classed as sound.

merchants; it only refers to their choosing to leave them be.[140] The prohibition on the killing of elderly men has been narrated to us from al-Hasan, Mujahid and al-Dahhak, but the Mujahid and al-Dahhak narration is not sound because it is by way of Juwaybir and Layth ibn Abi Sulaym. Similarly, this report from Abu Bakr also is unsound because it is from Yahya ibn Sa'id, 'Ata' and Thabit ibn al-Hajjaj, all of whom were born sometime after the death of Abu Bakr – may Allah be pleased with him. Likewise, the narration by a chain that includes al-Hajjaj ibn Artah who, in terms of his reliability, is irredeemable. If we wanted to argue on the basis of the report of al-Hasan, from Samurah, from the Prophet PBUH, and on the basis of the report whose chain includes al-Hajjaj, "Slay the older men of the associators and let their prepubescent youth remain,"[141] then we would definitely have been misled due to them. However, Allah, the Mighty and Majestic, has urged us to seek protection from arguing on the basis of what we do not consider correct, while the Qur'an and authentic Sunnahs are sufficient.

C17/7 As for their saying, "We only slay those who fight," it is baseless. Rather, we slay every one of them who is called to Islam until he either believes or gives *jizyah* in tribute, if he is of the People of the Book, as Allah has commanded in the Qur'an, not as Abu Hanifah commanded when he said, "If a woman reverts to disbelief, she is not slain;[142] but if she kills someone, she is to be killed. However, if the associators of those under a guarantee of Muslim protection insult the Prophet PBUH, they are to be left, despite their insulting him, so that they may get it off their chests and the Muslims may be belittled because of it." Perish this statement and whoever says it!

---

140 Ibn Hazm here makes a fair jurisprudential point that even a sound report of an observed practice does not have the force of a lawful command to act in a particular way.

141 Other chains of transmission exist that have been classed authentic.

142 This doctrine is attributed to Abu Hanifah in the works of members of the Hanafi school of law. However, based on a search of the *Maktabah Shamilah* database of Arabic-Islamic texts, it is not clear what the basis is of Ibn Hazm's claim that Abu Hanifah taught that protected non-Muslims were free to insult the Prophet PBUH.

C17/8 It has been narrated to us[143] by way of Waki‘, Sufyan told us, ‘Abd al-Malik ibn Umayr al-Qurazi told us, ‘Atiyah al-Qurazi told us, saying, "On the day of the treachery of Banu Qurayzah, when whoever amongst the males had reached puberty was slain, and whoever had not was allowed to go, I was brought before Allah's Messenger PBUH; and I was amongst those who had not reached puberty." This is a general ruling from the Prophet PBUH, who did not spare the hirelings, the traders, the peasants or the frail elders; and this is also a definite sound consensus from the companions – may Allah be pleased with them – because, amongst the many incidents that occurred in Medina, it was not hidden from any of its population.[144] Also by way of Hammad ibn Salamah, whom both Ayyub al-Sikhtiyani and ‘Ubayd ibn ‘Umar informed from Nafi‘, from Aslam the freed slave of ‘Umar ibn al-Khattab, who said that ‘Umar ibn al-Khattab wrote to the commanders of the armies, "Let them not bring back to us any of those scum. Slay them, but only slay those males who have begun to shave; and do not kill children and women."[145] Also by way of Ibn Abi Shaybah, from Ibn Numayr, whom ‘Ubayd Allah ibn ‘Umar informed, from Nafi‘, from Ibn ‘Umar, who said that ‘Umar ibn al-Khattab wrote to his armies, "Do not slay women and children," but that they should slay whoever had begun to shave.

C17/9 So, here is ‘Umar – may Allah be pleased with him – making no exception of the elderly, nor of monks, nor of hirelings, nor of anybody except women and children. Nor is there a sound report of any of the companions opposing him. Durayd ibn al-Simmah was slain, and he was a frail old man whose mind had become confused; yet the Prophet PBUH did not

143 Having expressed his opinion on the position that he opposes, namely that only combatants should be slain, Ibn Hazm presents evidence apparently to justify the indiscriminate killing of any male from the Muslims' enemies who has reached puberty.

144 What Ibn Hazm appears argue here is that the situation in Medina after the Hijrah or emigration, when the other religious and tribal groups entered into a mutual defence pact with the new Muslim community led by the Prophet PBUH, is analogous to that of conquered peoples whose status is protected under Muslim rule upon payment of the *jizyah*, and therefore that the same penalty that was applied to Banu Qurayzah for their communal act of treachery in the Battle of the Trench (5/627), apparently in conformity with the Torah (Deut. 20), should also apply to protected non-Muslims for individual acts of blasphemy.

145 This appears to be a paraphrase of one of several sound traditions from ‘Umar.

denounce his killing. Some have said, "It was because of his strategic thinking." So, we say to them, "Who is it who categorised for you those who possessed a capacity for strategic thinking apart from others? He should neither be heard nor obeyed."[146] Such categorisations as these should only be taken from the Qur'an or from the Prophet PBUH.[147] And, in Allah the Exalted, we place our trust.

146 Whilst Ibn Hazm may appear correct, based solely on the authentic hadiths in *Sahih al-Bukhari* and *Sahih Muslim*, there are other sound hadiths quoted in the commentaries to those two collections (e.g. *'Umdat al-qari'* by al-'Ayni) that indicate that, although Durayd was too old to fight, he did, indeed, play some strategic role in the Battle of Hunayn (8/630), commanding a force of 600, even if only symbolically as a figurehead.

147 This is exactly the point made by al-Qurtubi in his commentary on Q.9:5 (see para. A3/22 in the appendix below) to prove the opposite, namely that "His Exalted saying *{then slay the associators}* is linguistically general on every associator though, as explained previously in *Surat al-Baqarah*, the Sunnah made exceptions of women, monks, children and others." Clearly, both scholars cannot be right. Either (a) the Sunnah supports the indiscriminate killing of non-Muslims, according to Ibn Hazm's Zahiri doctrine; or (b) the Sunnah does not support the indiscriminate killing of non-Muslims. This latter alternative (b) is not only that of al-Qurtubi, but also of all the other famous Sunni jurists whose works Daesh propagandists plundered to extract the twenty-one misleading soundbites reproduced here in context.

Soundbite 18: "Be patient, Abu Jandal, for they are merely *mushrikeen*..."

UMAR BIN KHATTAB (R) SAID, ENCOURAGING ABU JANDAL TO KILL HIS OWN FATHER, SUHAYL IBN AMR, "BE PATIENT, ABU JANDAL, FOR THEY ARE MERELY MUSHRIKEEN & THEIR BLOOD IS NOTHING BUT LIKE THE BLOOD OF A DOG."-AHMED[148]

C18/1 Yazid ibn Harun told us, Muhammad ibn Ishaq ibn Yasar informed us, from al-Zuhri Muhammad ibn Muslim ibn Shihab, from 'Urwah ibn al-Zubayr, from al-Miswar ibn Makhzamah and Marwan ibn al-Hakam, who both said that Allah's Messenger PBUH set out in the year of the treaty of al-Hudaybiyah, intending to visit the Sacred House in Mecca, and not desiring to fight. He drove with him seventy camels for sacrifice, and there were seven hundred men also; so each camel was for ten men. Allah's Messenger PBUH carried on until 'Usfan, where Bishr ibn Sufyan al-Ka'bi met him, saying, "O Messenger of Allah, Quraysh has heard of your coming, and has set out with young and old alike, wearing tiger skins, swearing to Allah that you will never enter Mecca by force. Khalid ibn al-Walid has advanced with their cavalry to a place called Kura' al-Ghamim. So, Allah's Messenger PBUH said, "Woe to Quraysh! Their lust for war has consumed them. Why can't they just leave me and the rest of the people alone? If they were to harm me, that's what Quraysh want; and if Allah were to grant me victory, they would enter Islam in droves. And if not, they would fight with what strength they have. What are Quraysh thinking? By Allah, I will continue to struggle against them over what Allah has sent me to do until either Allah makes it victorious, or this neck has been separated." Then he commanded the people to go right between the two banks of acidic pasture on a route that comes out between the al-Mirar pass and al-Hudaybiyah, below Mecca. So, with the company of Muslims, he took that route. When the Quraysh cavalry saw from the dust thrown up by the company of Muslims that they had taken a different route, they withdrew to rejoin the rest of the Quraysh

148 See https://shamela.ws/book/25794/15420 (viewed 27/05/2025) for the Arabic text of *Musnad Ahmad*, hadith no. 18910, *Haddathana Yazid ibn Harun... 'an al-Miswar ibn Makhramah wa-Marwan ibn al-Hakam qala kharaja Rasul Allah* PBUH *'am al-Hudaybiyah*. It is classed as sound despite including the narrator Muhammad ibn Ishaq, who has been labelled *mudallis*, or deliberately obscure.

force. Allah's Messenger PBUH carried on till, he reached the al-Mirar pass, where his she-camel knelt down, and people said, "She's stubborn." Allah's Messenger PBUH said, "She hasn't become stubborn, that isn't her nature; rather He Who held back the elephants from Mecca is holding her back. By Allah, whatever plan Quraysh invite me for today, if they ask in it for maintaining kinship ties, I'll grant them it." Then he told the people, "Go down into the valley." They replied, "O Messenger of Allah, there's no water in the valley for people to head for." So, Allah's Messenger PBUH took an arrow from his quiver and gave it to one of his companions. The arrow went down one of those wells, and then the fresh water gushed forth until people's thirst was quenched. When Allah's Messenger PBUH was reassured, along came Budayl ibn Warqa' amongst some men of the Khuza'ah tribe, and he PBUH told them the same as he'd told Bushayr ibn Sufyan. So, they returned to Quraysh and said, "O men of Quraysh, you're being hasty with Muhammad. Muhammad hasn't come to fight. He's only come to visit this Ancient House, showing it all due respect," but Quraysh were suspicious of them. Muhammad – meaning Ibn Ishaq[149] – said that al-Zuhri said, "The Khuza'ah tribe, both its Muslims and its associators, were secretly supportive of Allah's Messenger PBUH, not hiding from him anything that was happening in Mecca. Quraysh said, "Even if that is all that he has come for then, by Allah, he will never enter it using force against us, nor must the Arabs speak of this." Then they sent Mikraz ibn Hafs ibn al-Akhyaf, a member of the clan of Banu Lu'ayy, to him. When Allah's Messenger PBUH saw him, he said, "This is a treacherous man." On reaching Allah's Messenger PBUH, Allah's Messenger PBUH spoke to him in much the same way as he had already spoken to Mikraz's fellows; then he returned to Quraysh and informed them of what Allah's Messenger PBUH had told him. Then they sent al-Hils ibn 'Aqlamah al-Kinani, who at that time was the chief of the Ahabish clan. When Allah's Messenger PBUH saw him, he said, "This man is from a community that worship God, so send the sacrificial animals out in front of him." So, they sent out the sacrificial animals; and when al-Hils saw the animals in their garlands drifting towards him across the breadth of

149 Ibn Ishaq (d.151/769) wrote the first biography of the Prophet Muhammad PBUH.

the valley, having gnawed away at their ropes from having been kept so long in that place, he returned without seeing Allah's Messenger PBUH out of amazement at what he'd seen, and he said, "O men of Quraysh, I have seen what it is not right to block, sacrificial animals in their garlands that have gnawed away at their ropes from having been kept so long in that place." So, they told him, "Sit down. You're a Bedouin. You have no knowledge." Then they sent to him 'Urwah ibn Mas'ud al-Thaqafi, who said to them, "O men of Quraysh, I've seen what whoever you send to Muhammad experiences in terms of abuse and foul language when he comes back to you. You also know that you are like a parent to me, and I am like a child to you, and that I've listened to those who have acted on your behalf. I have gathered together those of my people who obey me and have come to assist you in person." "You've spoken the truth," they replied. "We do not suspect you of wanting us harm." So, he set off until he came to Allah's Messenger PBUH and sat in front of him, saying, "O Muhammad, you've gathered the dregs of society, then you've brought them to your hometown to settle a score. Yet Quraysh have come forth bringing with them the she-camels with their young and wearing tiger skins, and they have entered into a covenant with Allah that you shall never pressure them into letting you enter Mecca. By Allah, to me, it's as though these companions of yours will run off and leave you tomorrow." Abu Bakr al-Siddiq, who was sitting behind Allah's Messenger PBUH, said, "Suck the idol al-Lat's cunt! [150] Would we run off and leave him?" 'Urwah asked, "Who's that man, O Muhammad?" He said, "He's the son of Abu Quhafah." 'Urwah said, "By Allah, if it weren't for a favour that you did me which I haven't repaid, I'd answer you back. But let this be in return for that." Then he took hold of the beard of Allah's Messenger PBUH. So, al-Mughirah ibn Shu'bah, who was in armour, standing guard over Allah's Messenger PBUH, pushed 'Urwah's hand away, saying, "Keep your hand off the beard of Allah's Messenger PBUH before – by Allah – it ceases to be

150 The word in the Arabic text literally means 'clitoris'. The question arises: Does this offensive exclamation by Abu Bakr represent a 'sunnah' of a companion who became one of the Prophet's PBUH rightly guided caliphs or successors, and hence a practice to be followed; or was it an out-of-character exclamation in breach of the clear instruction in Q.6:108 against insulting whatever other people worship apart from God?

joined to you." "Fie on you!" said 'Urwah, "What's got you all angry and impolite?" So, Allah's Messenger PBUH smiled. "Who's this, O Muhammad?" asked 'Urwah. The Prophet PBUH replied, "This is your brother's son, al-Mughirah ibn Shu'bah." "Have you turned traitor?" asked 'Urwah, "Wasn't it only yesterday that you began washing your own private parts?"

C18/2 The narrator then said that, after the insults aimed at al-Mughirah, Allah's Messenger PBUH said the same to 'Urwah as he'd said to his fellows before him, informing him that he had not come intent on war. Then 'Urwah left the place where Allah's Messenger PBUH was and saw how his companions behaved, and how he PBUH could scarcely perform his ablution without them vying over any drops of water that fell, or spit saliva except they did the same; nor would a single hair fall except they would seize it. So, he returned to Quraysh and said, "O men of Quraysh, I have gone to Khosrau in his kingdom, and to Caesar and the Negus in theirs but – by Allah – I have never seen any king treated like Muhammad by his companions. I saw a group of people who would not give him up for anything ever. So, take your decision."

C18/3 The narrator then said that Allah's Messenger PBUH had previously sent Khirash ibn Umayyah al-Khuza'i to Mecca, giving him as a mount to ride one of his own camels known as al-Tha'lab (i.e. the fox). When he entered Mecca, some people of Quraysh hamstrung it and even wanted to kill Khirash, but the Ahabish clan prevented them doing so until Allah's Messenger PBUH came, calling 'Umar to send him to Mecca. 'Umar replied, "O Messenger of Allah PBUH, I fear for my own safety from Quraysh; and there's no one in Mecca from Banu 'Adi to protect me. Quraysh know of my hostility and wrath towards them. But let me point out to you a man who is more honourable than I, 'Uthman ibn 'Affan. So, Allah's Messenger PBUH called for him and sent him to Quraysh to inform them that he had not come to make war, but that he had come to visit this Ancient House, out of respect for its sanctity. 'Uthman set off for Mecca, and Aban ibn Sa'id ibn al-'As met him on the way. So, 'Uthman got off his mount, put Aban in front of him, while he rode behind; and Aban provided 'Uthman protection so that he could convey the message of Allah's Messenger PBUH. Then 'Uthman continued on his way until he came to Abu Sufyan and the noblemen of Quraysh, where he conveyed to them what Allah's Messenger PBUH had sent him to say. So, they told 'Uthman, "If you wish to circumambulate the Ancient House alone, do so." He replied, "I won't do it until Allah's Messenger PBUH does so." Quraysh held 'Uthman back with them, and the news reached Allah's Messenger PBUH that 'Uthman had been killed.

C18/4 The narrator, Muhammad ibn Ishaq said that al-Zuhri told him that Quraysh sent Suhayl ibn 'Amr, a member of Banu 'Amir ibn Lu'ayy, saying to him, "Go to Muhammad and negotiate with him; and there should not be in the treaty anything other than that he return from here this year. By Allah, let not the Arabs ever talk of him pressuring us into letting him enter." So, Suhayl ibn 'Amr came to him PBUH; and, as soon as the Prophet PBUH saw him, he said, "Sending this man means that the people want a treaty." When Suhayl finally reached Allah's Messenger PBUH, the two of them began to parley, taking a long time going over the terms, until an agreement emerged between them. When the matter had been finalised, and there was nothing left except writing it out, 'Umar ibn al-Khattab leapt up and came to Abu Bakr, saying, "Is he not Allah's Messenger PBUH? Are we not Muslims, and are they not associators?" Abu Bakr said, "Of course!" "Why then," 'Umar asked, "should we debase our religion?" Abu Bakr replied, "O 'Umar, take your chances while you can.[151] I bear witness that he is the Messenger of Allah." 'Umar responded, "I too bear witness." Then 'Umar came to Allah's Messenger PBUH and said, "O Messenger of Allah, are we not Muslims, and are they not associators?" "Of course!" the Prophet PBUH replied. "Why then," 'Umar asked, "should we debase our religion?" So, he said, "I am Allah's servant and Messenger. I will not go against His command, nor will He cause my downfall." Then, even years later, 'Umar said, "I have not ceased to fast, give in charity, to pray, and to free slaves due to what I did, out of fear of the words that I uttered that day, hoping that it would be good for me in the hereafter."

151 Literally, what Abu Bakr said was "Cling to the stirrup wherever it is," which in this context means something like the English proverb, "Make hay while the sun shines."

C18/5 The narrator then said that Allah's Messenger PBUH summoned 'Ali ibn Abi Talib, and said to him, "Write 'In the name of Allah, the Kind, the Merciful.'" Suhayl ibn 'Amr said, "I don't recognise this. Instead write, 'In Your name, O Allah.'" So, Allah's Messenger PBUH said to 'Ali, "Write, 'In Your name, O Allah. This is what Muhammad the Messenger of Allah has agreed with Suhayl ibn 'Amr.'" Then Suhayl ibn 'Amr said, "If I bore witness to you being Allah's Messenger, I wouldn't oppose you. Instead write, 'This is what Muhammad ibn 'Abd Allah and Suhayl ibn 'Amr have decided: [1] To cease warring for ten years, during which people will be safe, and they will abstain from fighting each other; [2] that whoever of his companions comes over to Allah's Messenger PBUH [152] without his legal guardian's permission will be returned to them, and that whoever comes over to Quraysh from those who are with Allah's Messenger PBUH will not be returned to him; [3] that there will be no secret ill will[153] between us; and [4] there will be neither clandestine nor openly hostile incursions into each other's territory.'" Amongst the terms that they agreed at the time of writing the contract was [5] that whoever wished to enter into a pact and allegiance with Muhammad could do so, and whoever wished to enter into a pact and allegiance with Quraysh could do so. The Khuza'ah tribe leapt at the opportunity, saying, "We are for a pact and allegiance with Muhammad," while Banu Bakr seized the opportunity to declare, "We are for a pact and allegiance with Quraysh." Another condition upon Allah's Messenger PBUH was [6] "that you return from us this year and that, when next year comes, we will vacate Mecca for you to enter it with your companions, residing there three days, bearing with you only the light weaponry of a rider, not entering except with swords sheathed." As Allah's Messenger PBUH was engaged in the writing of the contract, Abu Jandal ibn Suhayl ibn 'Amr appeared in irons, having escaped Mecca to make it to Allah's Messenger PBUH.

---

152 The inclusion of "Allah's Messenger PBUH" in the text suggests that this is a paraphrase of the treaty's actual wording, since it's clear Suhayl would not have agreed to this wording.

153 The Arabic text contains an idiom that literally means "securely sewn up or fastened storage sack" of the type in which people would put their most valuable possessions for safekeeping, and so metaphorically in this case a heart that conceals feelings of hatred and enmity and a secret desire to harm and undermine the terms of the treaty.

C18/6 The narrator said that the companions of Allah's Messenger PBUH had set out from Medina not doubting in achieving victory due to a vision that Allah's Messenger PBUH had seen. However, when they saw what they saw regarding the treaty and their return to Medina, and what Allah's Messenger PBUH had taken upon himself, a deep sense of disquiet entered into the Muslim people that they might be wiped out. On seeing Abu Jandal, Suhayl went up to him and struck his face; then he said, "O Muhammad, the matter between me and you was concluded before this person reached you." The Prophet PBUH replied, "You have spoken the truth." Then Suhayl went up to Abu Jandal and grabbed hold of him by the scruff of the neck. Abu Jandal shouted out as loudly as he could, "O gathering of Muslims, will you return me to the people of idolatry so that they may persecute me because of my religion?" The Muslim people's sense of evil foreboding only increased. Then Allah's Messenger PBUH said, "O Abu Jandal, be patient and reflect on the fact that Allah – may He be glorified – has prepared for you and those other powerless Muslims who are with you in Mecca release and a way out. We have concluded a treaty between us and the people of Mecca. We have given them our word on this, and they have given us theirs; and we will not double-cross them."

C18/7 The narrator stated that 'Umar ibn al-Khattab then rushed up to Abu Jandal, and began walking alongside him, saying, *"Be patient, Abu Jandal, for they are merely mushrikeen and their blood is nothing but like the blood of a dog."*[154]

---

154 Or, "Be patient, Abu Jandal, for they are merely associators, and the blood of any one of them is worth no more than the blood of a dog." This again shows how the Daesh propagandists have chosen to misguide vulnerable Muslims with their use of sources. These words of 'Umar are taken and quoted out of context to justify treating the indiscriminate killing of non-Muslims as a matter of no consequence. However, they come straight after a statement of the Prophet PBUH that a treaty has been concluded, and that Muslims do not act treacherously. If the soundbite chosen by the propagandists serves any purpose in context, it is surely to indicate the emotional effect of seeing a fellow Muslim led away back into captivity, not to abrogate the legal force of what the Prophet PBUH had just said. It is comparable to someone extracting the insult uttered earlier by Abu Bakr, the first of the Rightly Guided Caliphs, preceded by the hadith's chain of transmission (i.e. "Yazid ibn Harun related to us, Muhammad ibn Ishaq ibn Yasar informed us, from al-Zuhri Muhammad ibn Muslim ibn Shihab, from 'Urwah ibn al-Zubayr, from al-Miswar ibn Makhzamah and Marwan ibn al-Hakam, who both said that [...] Abu Bakr al-Siddiq, who was sitting behind Allah's Messenger PBUH, said, 'Suck al-Lat's cunt!'") in order to imply a general rule

The narrator added that 'Umar brought the hilt of his sword close to Abu Jandal, later telling how "I longed that Abu Jandal should seize the sword and strike his father with it."[155] However, the man held back from slaying his own father, and the moment passed without further incident.

C18/8 After Allah's Messenger PBUH and Suhayl had finished writing the treaty, and Allah's Messenger PBUH was praying in the consecrated state of the pilgrim, agitated as to how come out of it, Allah's Messenger PBUH got up and said, "O people, slaughter your sacrificial animals and shave your heads," but no one moved. He then repeated much the same, but no one moved; and again he repeated much the same, but no one moved. So, Allah's Messenger PBUH went back and entered into Umm Salamah's tent, saying, "O Umm Salamah, what is it with these people?" She replied, "O Messenger of Allah, that state that you have observed has entered them. Don't speak to a single one of them but proceed to your sacrificial animal, wherever it happens to be, slaughter it and shave your head. If you do that, the people will do likewise." So, Allah's Messenger PBUH went back out, not speaking to anyone until he came to his sacrificial animal and slaughtered it. Then he sat down and shaved, upon seeing which the people got up and slaughtered their sacrificial animals and shaved their heads.

C18/9 The narrator concluded, saying that it was when it was halfway between Mecca and Medina that *Surat al-Fath* was[156] revealed.

---

on how Muslims are supposed to address disbelievers. Whilst it is true that the decontextualised soundbites that the propagandists posted on social media are fair translations of phrases taken from the named texts by the named scholars, nonetheless what they represent are modern examples of what 'Ali ibn Abi Talib famously described in a hadith in *Sahih Muslim* as "A word of truth by which falsehood is intended" (*Kalimat haqq urida biha batil*).

155 For a legal opinion on patricide, see para. C10/16 from *Kitab al-Umm*, where Imam al-Shafi'i mentions that, on the day of the Battle of Uhud in 3/625, three years before the incident described here, the Prophet PBUH instructed Abu Bakr not to kill his father, who had remained an associator. As such, any reference to Abu 'Ubaydah ibn al-Jarrah, who fought and killed his own father at the Battle of Badr in 2/624, a year before the Prophet's PBUH prohibition at Uhud, is moot.

156 *Surat al-Fath* begins (Q.48:1-3) *{We have granted you a clear victory, so that Allah may forgive you whatever of your sins has occurred previously and subsequently, to complete His favour on you, and to guide you along a straight path; and so that Allah may grant you mighty support.}* This shows that true victory need not be military.

Soundbite 19: "& to attack them with fire and catapults…"

IMAM SHAYBANI [sic] (R) SAID, "& TO ATTACK THEM WITH FIRE & CATAPULTS & THIS INCLUDES DEMOLISHING THEIR HOMES & THROWING SNAKES & SCORPIONS UPON THEM EVEN IF WOMEN & CHILDREN ARE AMONGST THEM. "-SHARH MIHNAJ[157]

C19/1 "& it is permitted to besiege the disbelievers in their cities," forts, "and citadels,[158] and to channel water to flood them, **and to shoot at them with fire and catapults" and whatever is equivalent in meaning to that in terms of destroying their houses,** cutting off their water supply, **throwing snakes and scorpions at them, even if there are women and children amongst them** based on His Exalted statement (Q.9:5) *{and seize them and besiege them}* and in *Sahih al-Bukhari* and *Sahih Muslim* that he PBUH besieged the people of Taif, and al-Bayhaqi recorded that he PBUH aimed a catapult at them; and, by analogy, general destruction was intended thereby.[159]

157 See https://shamela.ws/book/11444/2758 (viewed 09/06/2025) for the Arabic text of *Mughni al-muhtaj ibn ma'rifat ma'ani alfaz al-Minhaj*, Muhammad ibn Ahmad al-Khatib al-Shirbini's (d.977/1570) commentary on *Wa-yajuzu hisar al-kuffar fi al-bilad* in al-Nawawi's *Minhaj al-talibin wa-'umdat al-muftin*. The attribution to al-Shaybani in the handwritten list of Daesh soundbites that I received was clearly a spelling mistake.

158 In other words, this has to do with any army besieging the defensive position of another armed force, not with attacks on members of the public going about their normal lives.

159 In line with the tradition of Islamic jurisprudence, the excerpt from al-Khatib al-Shirbini is effectively an expansion of al-Nawawi's abridged paraphrase of the following quotation from *Kitab al-Umm*:

> Al-Shafii said, "If the enemy takes up a fortified position on a mountain or in a fort, a trench, thorny ground, or with whatever else offers some fortification, then there is no harm in shooting at them with large or small catapults, hurling fire, scorpions, snakes or whatever they detest, or to flood them with water so that they drown, or to bog them down, regardless of whether or not they have with them children, women or monks, because the territory is not defended by belonging to Islam or by any covenant. Likewise, there is no harm in setting fire to their fruit-bearing and other trees or destroying their dwellings and whatever inanimate property they have. And if anyone asks, 'What is the evidence for what you describe when there are amongst them infants and women whom it is forbidden to kill?' the evidence for this is that Allah's Messenger PBUH aimed a large or small catapult at the people of Taif, and yet we know that there were women and infants amongst them; and also that Allah's Messenger PBUH cut down and set fire to the agricultural wealth of Banu al-Nadir." Abu Damrah Anas ibn 'Iyad informed us from Musa in 'Uqbah, from Nafi', from Ibn 'Umar that Allah's Messenger PBUH set fire to the agricultural wealth of Banu al-Nadir.

See https://shamela.ws/book/1655/1113 (viewed 27/05/2025) for the Arabic text of *Qala al-Shafi'i wa-idha tahassana al-'aduw fi al-jibal aw hisn*.

Soundbite 20: "& it is permitted to fire upon the *kuffar* with catapults…"

IBN QASIM (R) SAID, "& IT IS PERMITTED TO FIRE UPON THE KUFFAR WITH CATAPULTS, EVEN IF WOMEN, CHILDREN, OLD MEN & MONKS ARE KILLED UNINTENTIONALLY, BECAUSE OF THE IJMA CONCERNING THE PERMISSIBILITY OF TERRORISING THEM."[160]

and

Soundbite 21: "Terrorising is permitted by *ijma'* against all types of *kuffar*."

IBN RUSHD (R) SAID, "TERRORISING IS PERMITTED BY IJMA AGAINST ALL TYPES OF KUFFAR. "-AL HASHIYA ALA RAWDH

C20/1 "Nor is it permitted" to take fodder or firewood, or "to raid except with the commander's permission unless an enemy surprises them and they fear their fury,"[161] with the 'a' vowel after the letter 'l', meaning 'their evil' or 'their harm', because, in that case, the welfare of the Muslims rests in attacking them. **Attacking the disbelievers by night is permitted, as is shooting at them with catapults, even if children and the like* are unintentionally killed**. Nor is it permitted to slay children, women, hermaphrodites, monks, frail old men, those with chronic illnesses, the blind, if they are not involved in strategic or tactical decisions, in fighting or in incitement; but they become slaves on capture.

C20/2 * such as women, the elderly and monks because of the permissibility of using the tactic of shock and awe[162] against all associators. **As Ibn**

---

160 See https://shamela.ws/book/12216/1962 (viewed 27/05/2025) for the Arabic text of *Wa-la yajuzu al-ta'alluf wa-al-ihtitab wa-al-ghazw illa bi-idhnihi*. The 20th and 21st quotations both appear to be from the same section of this *hashiyah* or gloss by the 20th-century Saudi scholar, 'Abd al-Rahman ibn Muhammad ibn Qasim al-'Asimi al-Hanbali al-Najdi (d.1392/1972), on *al-Rawd al-murabba' sharh Zad al-mustaqni'*, a super-commentary by the Egyptian scholar, Mansur ibn Yunus al-Buhuti (d.1051/1641), on *Zad al-mustaqni' fi ikhtisar al-Muqni'* by Musa ibn Ahmad al-Hijjawi (d.968/1560), being an abridgement of *al-Muqni'*, one of the best-known manuals of Hanbali law, by Muwaffaq al-Din 'Abd Allah ibn Ahmad Ibn Qudamah (d.620/1223). They have therefore been presented together here. However, following this quotation is the relevant excerpt of Ibn Rushd's actual work from which soundbite no. 21 is paraphrased.

161 The Arabic word *kalab* literally means 'rabies'.

162 The dictionary root meanings of *nikayah*, translated above as 'shock and awe', include: to cause damage, to harm, to hurt, to injure, to vex, to annoy, to offend. So, the term 'terrorising' as

Rushd[163] said, "shock and awe is allowed on the basis of scholarly **consensus against all types of associators**, be they male or female, children or elderly, young or old, except for monks. One group was of the opinion that they should be left alone and not taken captive; rather, they should be left alone and not exposed either to killing or to enslavement due to his PBUH saying, 'Leave them and what they have confined themselves to,' and pursuant to the action of Abu Bakr." And, in *al-Insaf*,[164] "the author wrote, 'And if they use Muslims as human shields, it is not permitted to shoot at them except if there is fear for the safety of the Muslims, when they may be shot at, intending thereby to hit the disbelievers.' There is no dispute over this." Meanwhile, al-Qadi[165] said, "It is permissible to shoot at them at a time of war, because leaving off shooting at them would lead to jihad becoming void."

---

translated by the Daesh propagandist is an acceptable translation so long as it is understood to refer to an overwhelming show of force in order to instil fear in the entire population by the massing of troops on the borders, for example, or by the display and/or use of massively superior military hardware, thereby sapping the enemy of the will to put up any resistance. On this basis, it is questionable that even the 9/11 attack on the Twin Towers meet the criterion of the term *nikayah* because it failed either to provoke a surrender or to deter retaliation.

163 Rather than refer to *Bidayat al-mujtahid wa-nihayat al-muqtasid* by the philosopher and Maliki scholar, Abu al-Walid Muhammad ibn Ahmad Ibn Rushd (d.595/1198), it is clear from the reference to Ibn Qasim's *al-Hashiyah 'ala al-Murabba'* and from the wording that the Daesh propagandists chose to quote Ibn Rushd from this footnote on C20/1 above, marked by an asterisk, which paraphrases the scholar's actual words, translated in C21 below.

164 i.e. *al-Insaf fi ma'rifat al-rajih min al-khilaf* by the Hanbali scholar, 'Ali ibn Sulayman al-Mardawi (d.885/1480).

165 i.e. Abu Ya'la Muhammad ibn al-Husayn Ibn al-Farra' (d.458/1066)

Soundbite 21 in full: "As for what is permitted of shock and awe..."

IBN RUSHD (R) SAID, "TERRORISING IS PERMITTED BY IJMA AGAINST ALL TYPES OF KUFFAR." –AL HASHIYA ALA RAWDH[166]

C21/1 As for what is permitted of shock and awe against the enemy, the use of shock and awe is not unrelated to taking property, lives and captives, by which I mean enslavement[167] and seizing. **As for the shock and awe that** constitutes **enslavement, it is allowed on the basis of** scholarly **consensus against all types of associators,**[168] by which I mean male or female, children or elderly, young or old, except for monks. One group was of the opinion that monks should be left alone and not taken captive. However, the reason why they should be left alone and not exposed either to killing or to enslavement is due to Allah's Messenger's PBUH statement, 'So, leave them and what they have confined themselves to,' and pursuant to the action of Abu Bakr."

C21/2 Most scholars are agreed on the ruler's having discretion on captives regarding particular options that include: being magnanimous towards them; enslaving them; killing them; ransoming them; and imposing on them the *jizyah* tribute. One group has said that it is not permitted to kill a captive.

C21/3 Al-Hasan ibn Muhammad al-Tamimi related that it was a consensus of the Prophet's PBUH companions; and the reason for their differing was the apparent conflict between the verse with this meaning and actions, when comparing the literal meaning of the Book and his PBUH actions. That is because the apparent meaning of His Exalted saying (Q.47:4) *{Then, when you meet those who disbelieve in battle, smite their*

166 See https://shamela.ws/book/21739/390 (viewed 27/05/2025) for the Arabic text of *Wa-amma ma yajuzu min al-nikayah bil-'aduw fa-inna al-nikayah* from *Bidayat al-mujtahid wa-nihayat al-muqtasid* by Abu al-Walid Muhammad ibn Ahmad Ibn Rushd (d.595/1198)

167 Ibn Rushd felt the need to clarify the word 'captives' because the Arabic also means 'necks', as shown in the Qur'an quotation below.

168 This seems to be the sentence from which the propagandists' soundbite ("Terrorising is permitted by ijma against all types of kuffar") originates. A question arises as to the propagandists' reasons for equating the specific Arabic term *al-mushrikin* (lit. 'associators') with the far more general term *kuffar* (i.e. disbelievers) in their translation. Clearly, not all disbelievers associate other beings with God in divinity.

necks...} the whole verse,[169] is that, after taking captives, the ruler only has the right to show magnanimity or to ransom. Also His Exalted saying (Q.8:67) *{A prophet does not have the right to take captives until he has inflicted great losses in the land...}* the whole verse.[170] The reason for its revelation due to the captives at the Battle of Badr indicates that in battle killing is better than enslavement. As for him PBUH, he killed captives in more than one place, he showed magnanimity, and he enslaved women. Abu 'Ubayd related that he PBUH did not enslave free Arab males. The companions after him reached a consensus over enslaving the People of the Book, both male and female.

C21/4 Whoever considers that the specific verse on what to do with captives abrogates his PBUH action, that person says "A captive should not be killed." Whoever considers that the verse contains no mention of killing captives, and that the intention in it is not to restrict what may be done to captives, rather, he PBUH did it, and consequently it is an extra ruling to what is in the verse, and it reduces the scope for censure that arose due to the abandonment of killing the captives of the Battle of Badr;[171] that person says killing captives is permitted.

169 The whole of verse Q.47:4 reads *{Then, when you meet those who disbelieve in battle, smite their necks until, once you have inflicted heavy losses upon them, you secure their bonds and choose either magnanimity or ransom so that war may lay down its burdens. That is God's command. If Allah had so willed, He Himself would have gained victory over them. This way, however, He tests some of you against others; and as for those who are killed fighting in the way of Allah, He will never cause their deeds to be lost.}*

170 The whole of verse Q.8:67 reads *{A prophet does not have the right to take captives until he has inflicted heavy losses in the land. You desire the advantages of this world, while Allah desires for you the Hereafter; and Allah is Mighty, Wise.}*

171 It is important to note that neither Q.8:67 nor Q.47:4 (revealed in the year 2/624) talks of killing captives *per se*, but rather of not taking captives – for ransom – until after heavy losses have been inflicted on the enemy in battle. Both *Surat al-Anfal* (Q.8) and *Surat Muhammad* (Q.47) were revealed within a short period after the Battle of Badr, which occurred in the year 2/624. The suggestion that these two verses are open to interpretation as permitting the slaying of captives must be weighed against the evidence in an authentic hadith in *Sahih al-Bukhari* (no.4339), which records the Prophet's PBUH unambiguous disavowal of such an act ordered by Khalid ibn al-Walid when commander of an expedition against Banu Jadhimah in the year 8/630.

C21/5 Killing of enemy combatants is only permitted where a guarantee of safety does not yet exist, and there is no disagreement regarding this amongst Muslims. They only differ over whose guarantee of safety is permissible and whose is not. They all agree over the permissibility of the ruler's guarantee of safety; and the majority of scholars over the permissibility of a free Muslim man's guarantee of safety, except that Ibn al-Majishun[172] considered that it is dependent on the permission of the ruler. They disagree over the safety guarantee of a slave and that of a woman. The majority agree on its permissibility, whilst Ibn al-Majishun and Sahnun said that the safety guarantee of a woman is dependent on the permission of the ruler, and Abu Hanifah said that the safety guarantee of a slave is not permitted unless he engages in the fighting.

C21/6 The reason for their disagreement is the contradiction of the generalities with analogical reasoning. As for the generalities, the statement of him PBUH is that "The lifeblood of Muslims is of equal worth. The least of them can extend their protection. They are united against all other than Muslims like themselves." The generality of this hadith implies the validity of a Muslim slave's guarantee of safety. As for the contrary analogical argument to this, it is that among the conditions of guaranteeing safety is complete legal competence, and a slave is deficient due to his servitude. His servitude must therefore analogically have some negative impact on guaranteeing safety as it has on many legal rulings, so the rule's generality should by analogy be particularised.

C21/7 As for their disagreement over a woman's guarantee of safety, the reason lies in their disagreement over the intention behind the statement of him – upon whom be blessings and peace, "We grant safe passage to whomever you have granted safe passage, O Umm Hani'," and whether a woman is analogous to a man in that matter. That is because whoever understands his PBUH statement, "We grant safe passage to whomever

172 'Abd al-Malik ibn 'Abd al-'Aziz, known as Ibn al-Majishun, was taught by Malik ibn Anas, while Sahnun (d.240/854?) studied under some of Imam Malik's students, from whom he transcribed the famous compendium of Imam Malik's teachings, *al-Mudawwanah*.

you have granted safe passage, O Umm Hani'," as permitting her guarantee of safety, not as confirming its validity in and of itself, and hence that, if it had not been for his PBUH permitting that, it would not have been acted on, that person says, "A woman has no right to guarantee safety, except if the ruler permits it. By contrast, whoever understands from that that his PBUH endorsement of Umm Hani's guarantee of safety was on the basis that it had been enacted and was effective, not on the grounds that it was his PBUH permission that made its enactment valid, he states that a woman's guarantee of safety is permissible. Likewise, whoever considers a woman analogous to a man and considers there to be no difference between them in that regard, he will deem her guarantee of safety permissible. However, whoever considers a woman to be legally deficient compared to a man will not deem her guarantee of safety to be permissible. Whichever way one looks at it, it does not impact on enslavement but only on killing.[173] It may also be possible for us to categorise the disagreement over this with their disagreement over masculine plural terms, and whether they include women or not, by which I mean as regards legal custom.[174]

C21/8 As for the type of shock and awe that relates to lives, it has to do with killing; and there is no dispute amongst Muslims that it is permissible in war to kill associators who are adult male combatants. As for killing such people after taking them captive, there exists the above-mentioned dispute. Likewise, there is no dispute between the scholars on the impermissibility of killing of their children or of killing of their women so long as neither the woman nor the child engages in fighting. However, if a woman engages in fighting, then shedding her blood is allowed, and that is because it is established that he PBUH forbade the killing of women and children, saying in relation to a woman killed on the battlefield, "This woman was definitely not fighting."

---

173 In other words, according to Ibn Rushd, it was deemed permissible at his time to enslave those hostile disbelievers whose lives were secured by a guarantee of safety.

174 Compare this to the practice in some English-language contracts of including a clause "The masculine includes the feminine." This paragraph is also interesting as proof of the different opinions on the legal equality of men and women, at least amongst Ibn Rushd's contemporaries in the 6th/12th century.

C21/9 The scholars disagree over the inhabitants of monasteries who have secluded themselves from people, the blind, the chronically sick, old men who do not fight, lunatics, ploughmen, and hired labourers. Malik said, "The blind, the lunatic and monks should not be killed; and they should be left with enough of their wealth to live off." Likewise, according to Malik, the frail old man is not to be killed. Abu Hanifah and his companions said the same. Al-Thawri and al-Awza'i only said, "Old men are not killed." Al-Awza'i also said, "Ploughmen are not to be killed." Al-Shafi'i in the more correct statement from him, "All these categories may be killed."[175] The reason for these disagreements is that some traditions, in terms of their specificity, contradict the generality of the verse in the Book and of his PBUH well-established statement, "I was commanded to do battle with people until they say, 'There is no god but Allah,'" the whole hadith; and that is in relation to His Exalted saying (Q.9:5) *{So, when the sacred months have passed, slay the associators wherever you find them...}* requiring the killing of every associator, be he a monk or not. Likewise, his PBUH statement, "I was commanded to do battle with people until they say, 'There is no god but Allah.'"

C21/10 As for the traditions that have been found on letting these categories to live, amongst them are that which Dawud ibn al-Husayn narrated from 'Ikrimah, from Ibn 'Abbas, that the Prophet PBUH, when he sent his armies out, said, "Do not kill the residents of monasteries." Also amongst those traditions is what was narrated from Anas ibn Malik, from the Prophet PBUH, who said, "Do not kill frail old men, small children or women, and do not take more than your share of the booty," recorded by Abu Dawud. Similarly, what Malik narrated from Abu Bakr, that he said, "You will find people who claim to have secluded themselves for the sake of Allah. Leave them be and what they have secluded themselves for." Also on this narration, "and do not kill a woman, nor a child, nor a frail old man."

175 This refers only to categories not included in the abovementioned consensus that "there is no dispute between the scholars on the impermissibility of killing of their children or of killing of their women so long as neither the woman nor the child engages in fighting."

It seems that the most persuasive reason for the disagreement on this issue is the contradiction between (Q.2:190) *{& fight in the way of Allah those who fight you, but do not transgress. Allah dislikes transgressors}* and His Exalted saying (Q.9:5) *{So, when the sacred months have passed, slay the associators wherever you find them...}* the whole verse. Whoever considers that this latter verse abrogates His Exalted saying (Q.2:190) *{& fight in the way of Allah those who fight you}* because fighting was initially only permitted against those who fought, says that the Sword Verse (Q.9:5) is to be taken according to its general meaning.[176] Whoever considers that the ruling in His Exalted saying (Q.2:190) *{& fight in the way of Allah those who fight you}* remains binding and that it extends to all those types that do not fight, he sees it as an exception to the general meaning of the other.[177]

C21/11 Al-Shafi'i argued on the basis of Samurah's hadith that Allah's Messenger PBUH said, "Slay the older men of the associators and let their prepubescent youth remain."[178] According to him, the root cause for killing is nothing other than disbelief; and this pretext must be extended without exception to all disbelievers. As for whoever inclines to the opinion that ploughmen are not to be killed argues that on the basis of has been narrated from Zayd ibn Wahb, who said, "A letter came to us from 'Umar – may Allah be pleased with him – and in it he wrote, 'Do not withhold any of the booty. Do not act treacherously. Do not kill children. Be mindful of Allah regarding peasants.'" Also, in a hadith from Rabah ibn Rabi'ah, the prohibition has come down to us against killing associator day labourers. That is based on the fact that Rabah marched out with Allah's Messenger PBUH in one of his battles, and Rabah and the companions of Allah's Messenger PBUH passed by a woman who had been killed, and Allah's Messenger PBUH paused a while over her and

---

176 See the excerpt from Ibn Hazm's *al-Muhalla* above, from which Soundbite 17 was taken.

177 One such scholar is al-Qurtubi in *al-Jami' li-ahkam al-Qur'an*, commenting on the Sword Verse (Q.9:5), referred to in the introduction to the contextualised soundbites of *A bundle of twigs in not a tree*.

178 According to a previous excerpt (see para. C17/6), Ibn Hazm was of the opinion that there are questions as to the soundness of this hadith's transmission. Other scholars have similarly found the narration to be weak.

then said, "This woman was not fighting." Then he looked at the faces of the people with him and said to one of them, "Catch up with Khalid ibn al-Walid and tell him he must not kill children, day labourers or women." The whole reason behind the scholars' disagreement on this is their disagreement over the root cause for killing. Thus, whoever claims that the root cause for that is disbelief makes no exception of any of the associators; whereas whoever claims that the cause for that is the capacity to fight due to the prohibition on killing women, despite their being disbelievers, makes exceptions of whoever does not have the capacity to fight and of whoever does not prepare himself for battle, such as the peasant and the day labourer.

C21/12 The prohibition on mutilation is valid. The Muslims agree on the permissibility of killing enemy associators with weapons, but they disagree over burning them with fire. One group of scholars detest burning them with fire or attacking them with it; and that is 'Umar's stance, and it has been narrated from Malik. Sufyan al-Thawri, however, permitted it. Some of the scholars have said, "If the enemy initiates that, it is permissible for Muslims; but if not, not." The reason for the scholars' disagreement is the apparent contradiction between the general and particular meanings of the scriptural evidence. As for the general meaning, it is His Exalted saying (Q.9:5) *{So, slay the associators wherever you find them}*, which makes no exception of one type of killing over another type of killing. As for the particular meaning, it lies in what has been established that Allah's Messenger PBUH said of a man, "If you catch him, kill him but do not burn him with fire, for no one punishes with fire except the Lord of the Fire."

C21/13 Jurists generally have agreed on the permissibility of firing at fortresses with catapults regardless of whether there are women and children in them or not, because of what has come down to us that the Prophet PBUH aimed catapults at the people of Taif. As for when a fortress has in it Muslim captives or Muslim children, one group of jurists has said, "The commander should hold back from firing at them with catapults," and al-Awza'i said it too, whereas al-Layth said, "That is permissible." The evidence relied on by whoever does not permit it is His Exalted saying (Q.48:25) *{If they had been separated, We would surely have inflicted a painful torment on those amongst them who had disbelieved}* the whole verse. As for the jurist who does permit it, it is as though he has taken into account the strategic benefit of doing so. This is the extent of shock and awe that it is permissible to reach regarding the lives of enemy associators and their enslavement.

C21/14 As for the use of the shock and awe tactic that is permissible in relation to their property, including buildings, animals and plants, the scholars have differed over that. Malik permitted cutting down trees, including fruit-bearing trees, and destroying habitable structures, but he did not permit killing livestock or burning date palms. Al-Awza'i detested the cutting down of fruit-bearing trees and the destroying of habitable structures, be it a church or something other than that. Al-Shafi'i said, "Houses and trees may be burnt if the enemy associators use them as strongholds for defence," but he detested the destruction of houses and the cutting down of trees if they did not use them as strongholds. The reason for the scholars' disagreement is that the action of Abu Bakr on that issue goes against his PBUH action that has been established, when he PBUH set fire to the date palms of Banu al-Nadir. Also, it has been established that Abu Bakr said, "You must not cut down trees, and you must not destroy buildings." Whoever thinks that Abu Bakr did this only because he knew from him PBUH of the abrogation of that action, as it is not permissible for Abu Bakr to go against him PBUH despite knowing what he PBUH did, or he considers that his PBUH order was particular to Banu al-Nadir for the raid on them, he declares in favour of Abu Bakr's statement. Whoever relies upon his PBUH action and does not consider the statement or action of anyone else a proof, he declares in favour of setting fire to trees. Malik differentiated between animals and trees only because the killing of animals is deemed mutilation, and he was forbidden to mutilate; and also it has not come down to us that he PBUH killed animals.

C21/15 So, this is knowledge about how far it is permissible to go with shock and awe against disbelievers regarding their lives and property.[179]

> If you have found this book helpful, please remember in your prayers not only the Prophet [PBUH] first and foremost, who was sent with the truth before the Final Hour, but also all the scholars from whose works these excerpts have been taken, that they may be rewarded in accordance with accuracy of the conclusions they reached on their path to acquiring and communicating knowledge, not for any negative consequences arising from the misinterpretation of their words. Let us also pray for ourselves that God may unite us on the truth, showing us the truth for what it is and granting us to pursue it, and showing us falsehood for what it is and granting us to eschew it.

179 Having completed this whole section of Ibn Rushd's treatise, what is clear is that he was not recommending the use of indiscriminate violence. Rather, after first declaring the use of shock and awe as a matter of consensus, he was then proceeding to outline for the benefit of his highly trained readers what might and might not be included in the tactic, based on numerous points of scholarly dispute. For propagandists merely to take the initial statement as a soundbite without any qualification, leaving it to the angry, untutored reader to interpret it however he or she saw fit, may be seen as deliberately misleading.

Appendix

Below are additional excerpts referred to in the footnotes above.

A1/7 Issue:[180] He said, "Whoever enters enemy territory in safety should not cheat them of their property nor engage in usury with them." As for the prohibition on usury in non-Muslim territory, we have mentioned it under the chapter of usury, in addition to Allah's Exalted word *{and He prohibited usury}*, along with all verses and hadiths indicating that the prohibition of usury is general, covers usury in every place and time. Regarding cheating them, it is forbidden because they have granted him safety conditional on his desisting from cheating them and on keeping them safe from himself. Even if it is not mentioned verbally, nevertheless its meaning is understood as implied. For that reason, whoever comes to us from them and cheats us, he is deemed to have breached his promise. If this is established, then cheating them is not permitted since it would constitute betrayal, and betrayal is not approved in our religion. The Prophet PBUH said, "Muslims stand by their undertakings." So, if he cheats them, steals from them, or borrows anything, he must return what he took to its rightful owners. If its rightful owners come to the land of Islam, be it with a guarantee of safety or after accepting Islam, he must return it to them. If not, then he should send it to them because he took it in a way that was forbidden him. So, returning what he took is required just as if he had taken it from the property of a Muslim.

A3/22 Second,[181] His Exalted saying *{then slay the associators}* is linguistically general on every associator though, as explained previously in *Surat al-Baqarah*, the Sunnah made exceptions of women, monks, children and others. Allah the Exalted said concerning the People of the Book

---

180 See https://shamela.ws/book/6910/6840 (viewed 24/06/2025) for the Arabic text of *Mas'alah: Qala man dakhala ila ard al-'aduw bi-aman* from Ibn Qudamah's *al-Mughni*. It helps the reader better to understand what Ibn Taymiyah, who was also of the Hanbali school, had in mind in his response on how Muslims should interact with others in territories like Mardin where they lived and worshipped in safety under non-Muslim rule.

181 See https://shamela.ws/book/20855/3014 (viewed 24/06/2025) for the Arabic text of *al-Thaniyah qawluhu ta'ala {faqtulu al-mushrikin} 'amm fi kull mushrik* from al-Qurtubi's *al-Jami' li-ahkam al-Qur'an*.

(Q.9:29) *{until they pay the jizyah}*, however, making it possible that the term "associator" does not include the People of the Book, implied by the prohibition of taking *jizyah* from idol worshippers and others, as will be explained. Know also that the unrestricted sense of His words *{then slay the associators}* implies the permissibility of slaying them in whatever way, except that reports have been adduced prohibiting mutilation. However, it may be that, when Abu Bakr put some of the apostates to death by burning in fire, with stones, by casting off mountain summits, or by drowning in wells, it relates to the generality of the verse. Likewise, Ali's burning some of the apostates[182] may be tilting towards this train of thought, relying on the general meaning of the term. Allah knows best...

B2/2.1 *Chapter on the prohibition of punishing any creature with fire, even ants and the like*[183]

B2/2.2 Abu Hurayrah reported that "Allah's Messenger PBUH sent us on an expedition, saying, 'If you find so-and-so and so-and-so' – of two men of Quraysh whom he named – 'then burn them alive.' Then, as we were about to set off, Allah's Messenger PBUH said, 'I had ordered you to burn so-and-so and so-and-so alive, but no one but Allah should punish with fire; so, if you find them, slay them.'" Narrated by al-Bukhari.

B2/2.3 Ibn Mas'ud reported that "Once we were travelling with Allah's Messenger PBUH, and he had gone off to answer the call of nature, we saw a lark with two chicks. We took her two chicks, and she began to beat about with her wings. When the Prophet PBUH came back, he said, 'Who caused her distress over her offspring? Give her offspring back to her.' Then he saw an ants' nest that we had set fire to, so he said, 'Who set fire to this?' We replied, 'Us!' He said, 'It is not fitting for anyone except the Lord of the Fire to punish with fire.'" Narrated by Abu Dawud with an authentic transmission.

182 For more on the controversial issue of punishment by fire in this world, see the authentic hadith in the final excerpt (B2/21-3) in this Appendix.

183 See https://shamela.ws/book/2348/1796 (viewed 24/06/2025) for the Arabic text of *Bab tahrim al-ta'dhib bil-nar fi kull hayawan* from al-Nawawi's *Riyad al-salihin*.

Sample presentation based on Soundbite 18

the danger of quoting hadiths out of context

a resource produced by RV

former curator of Arabic and Muslim prison chaplain

What Daesh wants us to think

The following slide shows a translation of words spoken by ‘Umar ibn al-Khattab, reported in a sound hadith from *Musnad Ahmad* on the Treaty of Hudaybiyah, which was concluded in the year 6/628. It is the 18th in a list of decontextualised soundbites selected and published by Daesh propagandists, apparently in its online magazine, *Dabiq*.

What Daesh wants us to think

18th soundbite: Umar ibn al-Khattab said, encouraging Abu Jandal to kill his own father, Suhayl ibn Amr, "**Be patient, Abu Jandal, for they are merely mushrikeen and their blood is nothing but like the blood of a dog.**" *Musnad Ahmad* (hadith no. 18910)

The word 'mushrikeen' means 'associators' of idols or other beings with God in divinity. For the purposes of Daesh propagandists, it is intended to be taken to mean any non-Muslim.

Questions

What do you think 'Umar hoped would happen?

What is likely to be the intention of Daesh propagandists in selecting this sentence?

Notes:
* 'Umar said this straight after the Treaty of Hudaybiyah was signed in 6/628.
* 'Umar later became the second of the Rightly Guided Caliphs.

What Daesh wants us to think – in its proper context

[…] Then Allah's Messenger PBUH said, "O Abu Jandal, be patient and reflect on the fact that Allah – may He be glorified – has prepared for you and those other powerless Muslims who are with you in Mecca release and a way out. We have concluded a treaty between us and the people of Mecca. We have given them our word on this, and they us; and we will not double-cross them." The narrator stated that then **'Umar ibn al-Khattab** rushed up to Abu Jandal and, walking alongside him, **said, "Be patient, Abu Jandal, for they are merely mushrikeen and their blood is nothing but like the blood of a dog."** The narrator added that 'Umar brought the hilt of his sword close to Abu Jandal, later telling how "I longed that Abu Jandal should seize the sword and strike his father with it." However, the man held back from slaying his own father, and the moment passed without further incident. […]

What Daesh wants us to think – in its proper context

[…] Then Allah's Messenger PBUH said, "O Abu Jandal, be patient and reflect on the fact that Allah – may He be glorified – has prepared for you and those other powerless Muslims who are with you in Mecca release and a way out. We have concluded a treaty between us and the people of Mecca. We have given them our word on this, and they us; and we will not double-cross them." The narrator stated that then **'Umar ibn al-Khattab** rushed up to Abu Jandal and, walking alongside him, **said, "Be patient, Abu Jandal, for they are merely mushrikeen and their blood is nothing but like the blood of a dog."** The narrator added that 'Umar brought the hilt of his sword close to Abu Jandal, later telling how "I longed that Abu Jandal should seize the sword and strike his father with it." However, the man held back from slaying his own father, and the moment passed without further incident. […]

What Daesh wants us to think – in its proper context

[…] Then ‘Umar came to Allah’s Messenger ﷺ and said, “O Messenger of Allah, are we not Muslims, and are they not associators?” “Of course!” the Prophet ﷺ replied. “Why then,” ‘Umar asked, “should we debase our religion?” So, he said, “I am Allah’s servant and Messenger. I will not go against His command, nor will He cause my downfall.” **Then**, even years later, **‘Umar said, “I have not ceased to fast, give in charity, to pray, and to free slaves due to what I did, out of fear of the words that I uttered that day, hoping that it would be good for me** in the hereafter**.** […]

Note: This is from elsewhere in the same hadith.

Questions

In its proper context, do you think that ‘Umar, when he looked back on the incident, was proud of what he’d suggested to Abu Jandal to do?

What words support your conclusion?

What Daesh wants us to think – in its proper context

The following slide shows an excerpt from *Kitab al-Umm* by Imam Muhammad ibn Idris al-Shafi'i (d.204/820), founder of the third surviving Sunni school of law. In all, Daesh propagandists took from this scholar's book three of the decontextualised soundbites in their list of twenty. This next short excerpt is from the broader context of the 10th soundbite in that list.

As you read the next quotation from Imam al-Shafi'i, ask yourself if it supports what 'Umar said to Abu Jandal.

What Daesh wants us to think – in its proper context

Imam al-Shafi'i said, "I detest that a man of the people of just cause should deliberately kill one of his kinsfolk from amongst the people of rebellion. Moreover, if he should hold back from killing his father, one of his kinsfolk or his brother from amongst the associators, I do not detest him doing that; rather I love him for it. That is because the Prophet PBUH held Abu Hudhayfah ibn 'Utbah back from killing his father and also Abu Bakr, on the day of Uhud, from killing his father."

Note: The Battle of Uhud (3/625), mentioned by Imam al-Shafi'i, was fought three years before 'Umar ibn al-Khattab urged Abu Jandal to kill his father after the signing of the Treaty of Hudaybiyah (6/628). Both Abu Bakr and 'Umar were among the closest companions of the Prophet ﷺ and close friends of each other.

What Daesh wants us to think – in its proper context

As revealed in *Surat al-Nisa'* (Q.4:92): *{"& it is not right for a believer to kill another believer except by mistake. Whoever kills a believer by mistake, then freeing a believing slave is a must and blood money handed to the family of the victim, unless they waive it out of charity. If the victim is from a people who are your enemy, and he is a believer, then freeing a believing slave is a must.* ***If he is from a people between you and whom there is a treaty, then blood money*** *must be* ***handed to the*** *victim's* ***family and the freeing of a believing slave.*** *Whoever does not find the means to pay, then fasting two consecutive months to repent from Allah. Allah is All-knowing, Wise."}*

Note: *Surat al-Nisa'* was revealed after the Battle of Uhud, so three years before the treaty. The verse above explains how to compensate and atone for a death by misadventure, not deliberate homicide.

What Daesh wants us to think – in its proper context

By contrast with the hostile disbeliever from enemy territory spotted marauding in Muslim-controlled territory, it is reported in *Sahih al-Bukhari* from 'Abd Allah ibn 'Amr that the Prophet PBUH said: **"Whoever kills a non-Muslim who has been granted a guarantee of protection, he shall not smell the fragrance of Paradise even though its scent wafts for as far as one can travel in forty years."**

Note: The safety of Suhayl ibn 'Amr, the father of Abu Jandal, would have been guaranteed by the Hudaybiyah Treaty, whose terms he had just negotiated and agreed.

List of authors and works from which the soundbites were extracted

Ibn Abi Zayd al-Qayrawani, 'Abd Allah ibn 'Abd al-Rahman (d.386/996)
al-Nawadir wa-al-ziyadat 'alá ma fi al-Mudawwanah [...] no. 7

Ibn Hajar al-'Asqalani, Ahmad ibn 'Ali (d.852/1449)
Fath al-Bari sharh Sahih al-Bukhari no. 12

Ibn Hanbal, Ahmad ibn Muhammad (d.241/855)
Musnad Ahmad no. 18

Ibn Hazm, 'Ali ibn Ahmad (d.456/1064)
al-Muhallá bil-athar no. 17

Ibn Muflih, Burhan al-Din Ibrahim ibn Muhammad (d.884/1479)
al-Mubdi' fi sharh al-Muqni' no. 15

Ibn Qasim, 'Abd al-Rahman ibn Muhammad (d.1392/1972)
al-Hashiyah 'ala al-Rawd al-murabba' sharh Zad al-mustaqni' no. 20

Ibn Qudamah, Muwaffaq al-Din 'Abd Allah ibn Ahmad (d.620/1223)
al-Kafi fi fiqh al-Imam Ahmad no. 8
al-Mughni no. 16

Ibn Rushd, Abu al-Walid Muhammad ibn Ahmad (d.595/1198)
Bidayat al-mujtahid wa-nihayat al-muqtasid no. 21

Ibn Taymiyah, Ahmad ibn 'Abd al-Halim (d.728/1328)
Majmu' al-fatawa nos. 4, 5

al-Mawardi, 'Ali ibn Muhammad (d.450/1058)
al-Hawi al-kabir no. 14

Muslim ibn al-Hajjaj (d.261/875)
Sahih Muslim no. 1

al-Nawawi, Abu Zakariya Muhyi al-Din Yahya ibn Sharaf (d.676/1277)
al-Minhaj sharh Sahih Muslim ibn al-Hajjaj no. 1

Concluding thought

Most readers will already have grasped through their own experience that the purpose of taking phrases out of their intended place is less often to enlighten than to deceive. As Muslims, the Qur'an (Q.4:41) warns us of the dangers of this practice, and the Sunnah (*Sahih al-Bukhari*, 7320) reminds us that we are just as likely to fall into this trap as those with scriptures older than our own. Some of us will therefore continue to wrongly interpret Islam and to believe such interpretations. Is this really a surprise given that, in secular matters too, and despite knowing the risks, people have not stopped giving out sensitive personal information to scammers posing on the phone as employees of their bank or clicking on links in dodgy phishing emails from unknown senders? There is no panacea. It is part of the human condition occasionally to make bad decisions.

The mindset of those whose current visceral hatred already disposes them to support unquestioningly, not to condemn, the use of disproportionate and indiscriminate violence against the "Other" will not instantly be changed by exposure to a book like this. Such people, be they Muslim or non-Muslim, will go through these excerpts with a metaphorical highlighter pen, marking for special attention only the same phrases picked out by the propagandists.

However, most people are not like that. Most people are not capable of sustaining a level of hatred that alienates them from any sense of empathy for the suffering of other humans, not matter how different from themselves they may be. For members of the often silent majority of humanity, Muslim and non-Muslim alike, reading these soundbites in context should give them the reassurance they need to trust that their gut instinct is correct, and that Islam is not a death cult, even though a few of its adherents choose to act as though it is. So, this volume is chiefly for them and also for those who have been radicalised, but the flames of their hatred have died down, and they are wondering whether to stoke the remaining embers or not.

There is an Arabic proverb that has been expropriated by Muslim extremists: *al-Haqq ablaja, wa-al-batil lajlaja* (i.e. "Truth shines brightly, whilst falsehood is repetitive and dreary"). What the twenty-one decontextualised soundbites in this book were presumably intended to do was to give the impression that the Daesh message, namely that the indiscriminate killing of non-Muslims and, indeed, many Muslims is without doubt true, and hence Sharia-compliant, because it seems to shine as clear as day from words found in the books of renowned scholars of the past. Conversely, the arguments to prove otherwise by imams preaching at Friday prayers in mosques, even if they do include a wealth of carefully selected quotations from the Qur'an and Sunnah, may come across not only as passive but also boring, demanding too long an attention span of fellow Muslims whose limited functional literacy and exposure to Islamic education make them vulnerable to such unspiritual, ideological propaganda.

By recontextualising each of the Daesh propagandists' soundbites, what becomes clear is that the mediaeval scholars were not arguing in favour of actions similar to those carried out by individuals in the name of Daesh, or for which Daesh claims responsibility. If the quotations had been intended as expressions of a general rule on the treatment of non-Muslims in war, one would rightly have expected those taken from comprehensive manuals of law to have come from the major sections of their works dealing with the waging of war rather than from, for example, a chapter on the recovering of stolen property. The one exception relates to Quotation 17, where the context makes clear that Ibn Hazm (d.456/1064) chose to stick to the absolutely literal meaning of the words of the Sword Verse (Q.9:5), in accordance with the approach of the now long defunct Zahiri school of law to which he belonged, and to ignore both its historical context and the evidence of the Sunnah to the contrary.

What is abundantly clear from the carefully constructed legal arguments presented in this volume is that none of scholars, not even Ibn Hazm, wrote with the intention of providing cynical Arabic-speaking extremists the means to incite mostly young hotheads with little, if any, formal Islamic education to commit atrocities. The ability to concentrate long enough to get the gist of a few soundbites in translation does not make anyone an *alim* or scholar, licensed to rule that Islam not only permits but, indeed, encourages Muslims to travel in safety to a public place and there to attack and kill unarmed fellow members of the societies in which they themselves were born and raised, or which had granted them residence.

May God guide us from darkness into light.

www.ingramcontent.com/pod-product-compliance
Ingram Content Group UK Ltd.
Pitfield, Milton Keynes, MK11 3LW, UK
UKHW050103160126
467039UK00009B/100

9 781836 154105